ALLEN CARR

Allen Carr was a chain-smoker for over 30 years. In 1983, after countless failed attempts to quit, he went from 100 cigarettes a day to zero without suffering withdrawal pangs, without using willpower and without putting on weight. He realised that he had discovered what the world had been waiting for – the Easy Way to Stop Smoking, and embarked on a mission to help cure the world's smokers.

As a result of the phenomenal success of his method, he gained an international reputation as the world's leading expert on stopping smoking and his network of clinics now spans the globe. His first book, *Allen Carr's Easy Way to Stop Smoking*, has sold over 12 million copies, remains a global bestseller and has been published in over forty different languages. Hundreds of thousands of smokers have successfully quit at Allen Carr's Easyway Clinics where, with a success rate of over 90%, he guarantees you'll find it easy to stop or your money back.

Allen Carr's Easyway method has been successfully applied to a host of issues including weight control, alcohol and other addictions and fears. A list of Allen Carr clinics appears at the back of this book. Should you require any assistance or if you have any questions, please do not hesitate to contact your nearest clinic.

For more information about Allen Carr's Easyway, please visit
www.allencarr.com

Allen Carr

The easy way to
stop
gambling

ARCTURUS

To Paul and the other gamblers of the world... at last there is real help at hand.

This book is based on the principles discovered by Allen Carr through his Easyway method, and developed by him in close collaboration with Robin Hayley, Chairman of Allen Carr's Easyway organisation and the most senior Allen Carr's Easyway therapist in the world. Having worked closely together across three decades, Allen entrusted Robin with the future development of the Easyway method to ensure that his legacy would achieve its full potential.

With editorial contributions from Tim Glynne-Jones

ARCTURUS

This edition published in 2018 by Arcturus Publishing Limited
26/27 Bickels Yard, 151–153 Bermondsey Street,
London SE1 3HA

ISBN: 978-1-78212-448-1
AD002711UK

Printed in the UK

What the media say about
Allen Carr's Easyway

'I was exhilarated by a new sense of freedom.'
The Independent

'A different approach. A stunning success.'
The Sun

'His skill is in removing the psychological dependence.'
Sunday Times

'Allow Allen Carr to help you escape today.'
The Observer

'An intelligent and original method!'
London Evening Standard

'For the first time in my adult life I am free.'
Woman's Journal

'I reckon this method is as close to foolproof as it gets.'
Time Out

'The Allen Carr method is totally unique in its approach.'
GQ magazine

Allen Carr's Easyway

The key that will set you free

CONTENTS

INTRODUCTION

Gambling is the fastest-growing addiction of the 21st century. The spread of the internet has driven a boom in the gambling industry, while governments have relaxed laws to allow more freedom to advertise and betting firms have developed ever-increasing ways for us to gamble. With this boom has come an exponential growth in the number of people who find themselves trapped in the misery of gambling addiction.

The compulsion to gamble can be devastating. It can disrupt your work life, your social life, put intolerable strain on relationships, destroy your finances, lead to ill health, mental breakdown and, in some cases, even suicide. But even when we know it's ruining our life and would love to be free of it, escape can seem impossible.

Why? Because we think there's only one way out: the hard way. The common understanding is that addictions such as gambling, smoking and alcoholism can't be conquered without tremendous willpower, suffering and deprivation. But I have good news for you, there is another way.

I discovered this for myself in 1989, when I went to Allen Carr's clinic in the hope that he could help me stop smoking. To my amazement I succeeded easily, painlessly and permanently. What I experienced with Allen was completely different to my previous attempts to quit by using willpower and nicotine gum. By the time we finished I knew I no longer had any desire to smoke and so I didn't need willpower.

From day one as a non-smoker I started enjoying social occasions more and handling stress better. There was no feeling of deprivation; on the contrary, I felt hugely relieved and elated that I was finally free.

I was so impressed with Allen Carr's method that I wrote to him asking if I could join his mission to cure the world of smoking. I was lucky enough to be accepted, and even luckier later to be appointed Managing Director of the company formed to spread the method all over the world.

Today more than 400,000 people have visited our clinics in over 45 countries around the world, and Allen Carr's books have sold more than 16 million copies, been translated into 42 languages and read by an estimated 30–40 million people in 57 different countries. This phenomenal success has been achieved entirely by word of mouth, through the personal recommendations of the millions of people who, like me, have succeeded with the method. Allen Carr's Easyway has spread all over the world for one reason alone: **BECAUSE IT WORKS.**

And it doesn't just work for smokers. Prior to becoming hooked on nicotine, I fought a continuous battle with my weight. I thought my tendency to binge, followed by crash diets, was down to a fault in my personality and I despaired at the thought of never being able to become free from the problem and happy about my weight.

That all changed when Allen showed me his first draft of *Allen Carr's Easyweigh to Lose Weight* and I realised he had found the solution to the problem that had plagued my whole life. As I read through the text, I found the powerful logic irrefutable. By the end, I knew that my weight problem was solved.

I was convinced there and then that Allen's method wasn't only effective for the obvious substance addictions: smoking, alcoholism and drug abuse; it could be applied successfully to any form of compulsive behaviour.

The Easy Way to Stop Gambling applies Allen Carr's Easyway method to one of the most devastating compulsions of all. In the last ten years alone, millions of people around the world have fallen into the clutches of gambling addiction, yet it is a condition that leaves you feeling completely alone.

Unlike any other addiction, it can wipe you out in a single day. Online gambling has made it possible to sit at home, in private, and literally gamble your life away. Sadly, more and more people are doing just that.

The Easy Way to Stop Gambling is the key that will set you free from this prison. It will completely change your mindset by stripping away all the illusions and fears that have prevented you from escaping the trap before. Easyway does not involve willpower or deprivation as it removes the desire to gamble and you will be able to look forward to enjoying the rest of your life free from the debilitating burden of being a slave to gambling.

Freedom from debt, from having to lie to your loved ones, your employer, yourself, freedom from self-loathing, from the sense of helplessness and slavery... all the freedoms you enjoyed before you got hooked on gambling will be yours again, regardless of who you are, where you come from or how much you gamble. Once you are in the right frame of mind, following the practical steps set out in this book to solve your problem will become easy.

Allen Carr's Easyway transformed my life. It can do the same for you.

Robin Hayley M.A. (Oxon), M.B.A., M.A.A.C.T.I.
Chairman, Allen Carr's Easyway (International) Ltd

Chapter 1

THE KEY

This book will enable you to stop gambling, immediately, painlessly and permanently, without the need for willpower or feeling any sense of deprivation or sacrifice.

Perhaps you find that claim a little too good to be true. I promise you that it's achievable, regardless of who you are or what your personal circumstances may be. All you need is an open mind.

This book is your friend, your confidant and your guide. It will take you on a journey that will lead you out of the gambling trap, but it will not judge you or embarrass you, nor will it put pressure on you to undergo painful measures. All I ask is that you keep an open mind and follow the instructions – do that and you cannot fail to escape. In fact, you'll find it easy.

Perhaps that goes against everything you've ever been told about problem gambling. But ask yourself this: has what you've been told before worked for you? If it had, you wouldn't be reading this book.

The truth is that it's not necessary for you to suffer the misery of gambling addiction. Nor is it necessary for you to suffer in order to free yourself and regain control of your life. In order to quit gambling, you need first to understand the nature of the problem and then to follow an effective method to solve it.

This book will enable you to do both by applying to your gambling problem a proven method for overcoming addiction that has worked for millions of people around the world.

DID YOU SAY ADDICTION?

There's a common misconception that addiction only applies to drugs such as nicotine, alcohol and heroin. But it's now widely accepted that addictions can also be behavioural, such as over-spending and over-eating. And the first behavioural addiction to be recognised as such was gambling.

Listen to gamblers talk about their problem and the language they use is that of the drug addict.

'It's like a high – a buzz.'

'It just hooks you right in – I can't escape.'

'One bet was all it took for me to be hooked again.'

'I knew I needed help, but I still didn't want to stop.'

'I stole money to finance my gambling.'

'I love gambling but hate being a gambler.'

'My wife, my kids, my home – nothing seemed as important as my next bet.'

As with substance addictions including smoking, alcoholism and other forms of drug abuse, problem gambling is a man-made condition, which starts small, seemingly under control, but soon grows to the point where it takes you over and destroys your life. You find yourself playing for bigger and bigger stakes and, as your losses increase, the only way you can see to recover is to gamble more. Even the occasional big win just feeds the addiction as the money inevitably finds its way back into the coffers of the bookmaker, the casino or the other players. You're falling deeper and deeper into a trap and you just can't see a way out.

A TWO-FACED PROBLEM

It's not just gambling addicts who have a twisted perception of gambling. Society as a whole can't seem to make up its mind as to whether gambling is good or bad. On the one hand there's the local vicar buying raffle tickets at the village fete, on the other there's the inveterate gambler who has squandered everything and destroyed his family. Why do we view the former with respect and the latter with scorn? Are they not both taking part in the same practice? At what point does gambling turn from being a force for good into being a force for evil?

The simple answer is that gambling becomes a problem the moment you believe that it can help you. As long as you believe that gambling is a way to make money, that with practice you can beat the odds, and that it can't become a problem if you only gamble what you can afford,

> then you are laying yourself open to one of the most
> severe forms of behavioural addiction.
>
>   Even with something as apparently innocuous as a
> local raffle, one truth remains constant: the one person
> guaranteed to win is the person selling the raffle tickets.
> When you understand the implications of that simple fact,
> you begin to see through all the other misconceptions
> about gambling.

Feeling unable to stop gambling despite the harm you know it's causing you is a sure sign of addiction. As with all addictions, it's the illusion that the behaviour provides a genuine pleasure or crutch that keeps you trapped. Smokers suffer the illusion that cigarettes help them relax. In fact, they do the complete opposite. All a cigarette does is partially and temporarily relieve the uncomfortable feeling of the body withdrawing from nicotine – a feeling that non-smokers do not suffer from in the first place.

As the nicotine leaves the body, smokers start to feel edgy and anxious. Because they're under the illusion that the only thing that will make them feel better is smoking, they reach for another cigarette. The reality is that the next cigarette will simply introduce more nicotine into the body, temporarily and partially relieving the symptoms of discomfort caused by withdrawal, guaranteeing that when that nicotine leaves the smoker's body, the smoker will again feel uptight and feel the urge for another cigarette. Non-smokers do not have this problem. Therefore,

SMOKERS SMOKE IN ORDER TO FEEL
LIKE NON-SMOKERS!

Similar misconceptions are at work when it comes to gambling. The illusion is that gambling makes you feel good, by providing a high or a feeling of wellbeing. In fact, all it's doing is restoring your levels of happiness and wellbeing to somewhere near normal, having already depleted them. I will explain how this depletion happens in greater detail later.

Put simply, the reason gambling addicts think gambling gives them a high is because during the act of gambling their withdrawal is alleviated and they get a fleeting taste of how a non-addict feels. In addition to this, while the card hand is being played, while the roulette wheel or the lottery balls are spinning, while the dogs or horses are running or the big game is being played, your mind becomes desensitised to the misery that gambling is causing you and you feel the sense of freedom and confidence that someone who isn't suffering the slavery of gambling addiction feels all the time. You momentarily stop feeling like someone who has lost – like a loser – and start feeling like a contender, like a potential winner. You briefly live in a moment of possibilities where you're not hamstrung by the side effects of your gambling addiction. In other words, for that very short period you feel like a non-gambler.

That illusory boost soon wears off and you're left feeling miserable again and guilty that now you're in even more trouble than before. However, because you regard gambling as the one thing that alleviates your misery, you go and gamble more. It's a vicious circle and the longer you go on labouring under the illusion that gambling gives you pleasure or a crutch, the further you descend into the trap and the more miserable you become. Like all addictions, it doesn't get better; it just gets worse and worse and ultimately you end up as the gambling equivalent of a chain-smoker, gambling constantly, day in, day out, not being able to stop. Isn't it that, or the fear of that, which has made you pick up this book? You don't need me to tell you that gambling is controlling you, you accepted that truth the moment you decided to do something about it.

IN HER OWN WORDS: DIANE

After I had my first child I gave up work and found myself at home alone a lot of the time. I started surfing the net, looking for things to keep me amused. I played a bit of low-stakes online poker just for fun, but soon I thought it would be more exciting if I stood the chance of winning something a bit more significant. Maybe it was because I wasn't earning any more, I somehow felt the need to make money.

Even though I was still only playing for relatively small stakes, I could feel it taking me over. It was hard work looking after our baby, but I comforted myself with the thought that as soon as I'd got him to sleep I could go online and play. The sad thing is, if he woke up when I was playing, it made me angry. The game was demanding my full concentration and I didn't want anything else getting in the way.

If I lost, I took it personally. I wanted to get back in there and win my money back. It was a matter of pride more than the actual money. I hated the thought that someone had outsmarted me or even that they'd had more luck than me. I wanted to settle the score and the only way to do that was to go and play again. The trouble was, every time I played I was raising the stakes, trying to turn my losses into winnings.

I started paying less and less attention to my baby, sometimes leaving him to cry while I played. Of course, I concealed it from my husband when he came home each day, but I found it harder and harder to take my mind off the game, even when he was around. If I was still playing when he came home, I would hurriedly quit the game, which irritated me and made me short-tempered with him. When he went to bed, I'd tell him I had one or two things to do and would get straight back into a game.

Our marriage became very rocky and I blamed him and the baby. I regarded the gambling as the one thing that could make me happy and I couldn't wait for him to leave for work each morning so I could get online. Of course, I now realise that the real cause of my misery was gambling itself.

IT'S NOT ABOUT THE MONEY

This book will help you unravel the illusions that trap you. It will help you to see that gambling does not relieve your misery, it's the cause of it.

Most adults have experienced what it feels like to gamble. Three-quarters of the adult population gamble regularly according to the British Gambling Survey of 2010. Even though the law applies similar restrictions to gambling as it does to smoking and drinking alcohol, the dangers of gambling aren't publicised in the same way. In fact, it's often dressed up as a bit of fun, in which, for a minimal risk, you could win a life-changing amount of money. Where's the harm in that?

The fact is there would be no problem if we *were* in control. We would be able to gamble only what we could afford to lose, only when we wanted to, and we would be able to stop whenever we chose. But that isn't the case, is

> *By gaming we lose both our time and treasure – two things most precious to the life of man.*
> **Owen Feltham (author)**

it? Whether we win or lose, the compulsion to keep gambling grows. When we lose, we feel driven to gamble again in a bid to recover our losses. When we win, we blow our winnings on more bets.

It's not the money that keeps us gambling but the belief that gambling gives us pleasure or a crutch. It's the same for all addictions. Gamblers talk about a 'high' – the thrill of chancing all on one throw of the dice. In fact, the more we gamble, the more we lose control.

It's safe to assume from the fact that you're reading this book that you do not feel in control. Perhaps you've tried to quit in the past and found you couldn't. No matter how hard you tried, you felt you lacked the willpower. Now you gamble even when part of you doesn't want to and you're powerless to stop.

In fact, as I will explain later,

YOU'RE NOT POWERLESS AND YOU DON'T LACK WILLPOWER

If you've made failed attempts to stop gambling in the past it's simply because you were following the wrong method.

IT'S TIME WE TALKED

Problem gambling is a devastating condition. In addition to the chronic financial trouble it brings, it can lead to severe anxiety, illness, other addictions, breakdowns in relationships and, in the most tragic cases, suicide. It should be the subject of regular, high-profile health warnings, yet we are encouraged to gamble on prime time TV all the time, and the subject of problem gambling is swept under the carpet. Even modern, apparently progressive, western governments have taken measures that encourage gambling on an epidemic scale. There's nothing like a taxable addiction to keep money rolling into government coffers without fear of the source drying up.

Have you ever been at a party when someone has had a nasty accident? One minute everybody's having fun, the next minute you're feeling shocked and frightened. It spoils the party. Problem gambling is the equivalent of that nasty accident, but it seems that the people with the power to help don't want to pay it any attention. Despite the fact that so many people develop gambling problems, billions of pounds, dollars, euros, and yen are being made by the gambling industry (and tax is levied by grateful governments) and they don't want anyone upsetting the apple cart.

That's why society prefers the image of gambling as presented by James Bond in *Casino Royale* to the reality of the guilt-ridden loser, who's desperately hoping for that one big win before their family discover that they're catastrophically in debt.

> **DEBT**
> Money worry is a devastating condition in its own right, regardless of whether it's caused by gambling or something else and the effects of problem gambling run far deeper than the money lost. For specific advice on solving financial worries, read *Allen Carr's Get Out of Debt Now.*

There are a number of common myths surrounding problem gambling:

It's only a problem for poor people.
Gambling doesn't just cause financial troubles. It also leads to breakdowns in relationships, depression, loss of work, crime and

suicide. The incidence of gambling increases with wealth and millions of wealthy people fall victim to gambling addiction. They lose everything. Former international soccer player, Paul Merson, summed it up when I asked him if he was jealous of the six-figure weekly pay packets enjoyed by modern-day English Premier League footballers. I asked him if his earnings had been that high, would he have had some of his fortune left? His reply says it all. 'I was seriously well paid as a footballer in my day, not nearly as much as modern-day players, but I'm not jealous of them. It wouldn't have made any difference if I was earning £100,000 per week like them, I would have still ended up giving it all straight to the bookmaker.'

Problem gambling means gambling every day.

Frequency varies among problem gamblers. Any gambling that causes a problem is problem gambling.

Problem gamblers are driven to it by difficult circumstances.

It can affect anyone in any walk of life. Problem gamblers tend to blame their circumstances, or other people, in order to justify their behaviour.

Problem gambling would not be such a tragedy if it was just about losing money. The real problem is the way it makes us feel when we know we are hooked. It's like Jekyll and Hyde: part of us knows that gambling is causing us and those close to us terrible harm, yet another part keeps compelling us to gamble, in the belief that it holds the solution to our problems.

It's a classic story: the problem gambler who's hit rock bottom and decides to blow his last possessions on one final bet. It could be the one that wipes out his debts and puts him back on his feet again, ready to carry on his life a new man, free from the torment he's been suffering as a gambling addict.

There are two problems with this:

1. The likelihood of him winning is far smaller than the likelihood of him losing everything.

2. If he does win, he will forever regard gambling as his saviour and will quickly fall back into its clutches again.

And yet it's these illusions that keep us gambling, despite feeling out of control, helpless and stupid. The constant cycle of hope and despair leaves us unfulfilled, empty and feeling like a failure. The more we fail to achieve the fulfilment we seek from gambling, the more compelling is the temptation to try again, even though we know deep down that it's futile. We become preoccupied and unable to enjoy life's simple pleasures.

Ashamed of our terrible lack of control, we try to hide the fact from our friends and loved ones, and so we become secretive, deceitful and evasive, which in turn makes us short-tempered, guilty and stressed.

KEEPING YOUR PROBLEM TO YOURSELF CREATES A BURDEN THAT ONLY MAKES IT HARDER TO ESCAPE FROM THE TRAP

This book will relieve your burden. It will show you that you're not alone and that your gambling problem has nothing to do with your character or personality. Regardless of your background and current circumstances, it will help you to get free from the awful effects of gambling that has run out of control: the nagging loss of self-confidence, the secrecy and dishonesty, the anger and defensiveness, the depression and desperation.

WAITING FOR A MIRACLE

'I knew I needed help, but I still didn't want to stop.' The gambling addict suffers from a constant tug-of-war. You know something is causing you harm and misery and threatening to destroy your life, yet you feel compelled to go on doing it. Every day the misery gets worse, yet the compulsion to go on gambling gets stronger. You know that the only sensible thing to do is quit, yet you suspect that quitting will be worse than carrying on because you still believe that your addiction gives you some kind of pleasure or crutch.

Most of the time you try to avoid involving anyone else in your addiction. Eventually, though, your money runs out and you're forced to borrow, perhaps from a friend or relation. You hope they'll be discreet and won't ask what it's for. If they do, you don't tell them it's to finance your gambling addiction. You make up some story – you lie to them – and when they come to ask for the money back, you become defensive and elusive.

People lose respect for you. They stop trusting you. Now you're putting far more than money at stake: you're risking friends, family, your job, your home, your entire life.

I'm not trying to scare you or paint a melodramatic picture of problem gambling and its consequences in the hope of frightening you into changing your ways. The chances are that you're already well aware of much of what I've mentioned so far. That's why you've picked up this book. But because of the chains that gambling addiction imposes on everyone it enslaves, you have until now felt powerless to do anything about it.

The sad fact is that some people actually end up taking their own life because of gambling addiction and the misery it causes can lead to other addictions, such as smoking, drinking and other drugs, which in turn affect your health and wealth and shorten your life.

The realisation that you're not, in fact, in control, and that gambling controls you, can quickly lead to despair. And often, in trying to protect your loved ones from the horrors that you're going through, in trying to keep them fed and clothed, sheltered and happy without them realising that you can no longer afford to, you run the risk of losing them altogether. Rather than face that horror, some people choose to take their own life. Such is the degree of despair and misjudgement that gambling addiction can instil.

Most gamblers, however, aren't driven to suicide. They go on enduring the misery, day after day, feeling helpless to do anything about it, just waiting for the day when some miracle occurs and they find they're no longer hooked.

YOU DON'T NEED A MIRACLE

All you need is to recognise that gambling is an addiction that provides you with no genuine pleasure or crutch, and then to follow a proven method to help you quit. This book will enable you to conquer your despair and make sound judgements, not only about gambling but also about your whole life. It will also enable you to live free from the constant anxiety of being found out.

There's no need for you to be miserable. The main aim of this book is to help you escape the misery of gambling addiction and find happiness. That means living without fear and panic. In short, living happily without gambling.

SLAVES TO THE MACHINE

It sounds like an urban myth but some gambling addicts wear nappies while they're playing slot machines so they never need to go to the bathroom. They hate getting up because they fear that someone else will take their place and win 'their' jackpot.

In a study conducted by Professor Tim Pelton for the University of Victoria's Center for Addiction, Canada, casino staff reported that they no longer bat an eyelid at customers wearing nappies. How do they know gamblers are wearing them? The answer is they can see them 'peeping out' of the clothing of seated patrons and they also find them discarded in large numbers in casino bathrooms.

The sad truth is that addicts only agonise about vacating their posts because they don't understand how slot machines work. No one's told them that random-number generators operate continuously in slot machines, running through dozens of combinations of digits at incredible speed. The chances of you putting in a coin or pressing a button at the same split-second as somebody else are infinitesimally small. So the fact that someone else hits the jackpot on 'your machine' doesn't mean you would have too!

YOU ARE NOT ALONE

What would you consider to be an acceptable level of gambling? Buying a lottery ticket each week? Going to bingo on a Friday night? Playing the slot machine in the pub at the weekend? Having a flutter on a horse race once a year?

Perhaps you envy people whose gambling does not exceed these levels. Perhaps you think there's no way you could get into the difficulties you're in now if that was the extent of your gambling.

But the truth is that all gambling is part of the same problem. When you buy a lottery ticket, you buy into the same illusion as the desperado who stakes his last dollar on a pair of twos. Many people become addicted to lotteries, despite the fact that the odds against winning are huge.

> **WHAT ARE THE ODDS?**
> Your chances of winning a lottery where you select six numbers from 49 and have to get all six right are approximately 14 million to one! This means that, if you buy a ticket once a week, on average you would win once every 270,000 years!

It's no coincidence that as gambling restrictions have been relaxed and opportunities to gamble made much easier to come by – particularly online – the incidence of problem gambling has risen dramatically. The rise in the number of women falling into the gambling trap is particularly alarming.

GAMBLING ADDICTION IS ONE OF THE MOST CATASTROPHIC EPIDEMICS OF THE 21ST CENTURY

Yet it's a very lonely condition. Society has made a taboo of talking about any problem that involves money, so regardless of how deeply we have sunk into the trap, we tend to feel we should solve our problem alone. The result is millions of people around the world suffering the same agony in silence. A close friend of mine has never once mentioned his gambling problem but it's still painful to witness. Even though he's constantly battling financial catastrophe and has now lost his home with everything in it, including his loving wife and children as a result of it, he remains entirely incapable of admitting he has a problem, let alone asking for help.

No matter how isolated you may feel, you are not alone. The ill effects of gambling are widespread and millions of others are experiencing exactly the same torture as you.

It's important to realise that your gambling problem isn't unique to you. There's nothing about your personal situation that makes gambling addiction inevitable.

The sad fact is that gambling addicts often succumb to other addictions, such as smoking or alcohol. You may interpret that to mean that certain types of people are susceptible to addiction, and assume that this applies to you.

Please put that thought out of your mind immediately. As I will explain in greater detail in the coming chapters, gambling addiction has nothing to do with the way we, as individuals, are made. Anyone can succumb to gambling addiction, regardless of genetic make-up, and anyone can succeed in quitting just as easily and painlessly.

Whoever you are, whatever you do, wherever you live, however much money you earn, you can find yourself trapped by gambling addiction and heading towards devastation. The good news is that you can get out of the trap just as easily as you got into it. And once you accept that gambling is an addiction, you can begin your escape.

America on the hook

If you recently visited a casino in the US, you're one of over 81 million people who did the same this year. That's more than the entire population of Britain. In 1982 Americans lost approximately $10 billion collectively on gambling. By 2016 that figure had multiplied by a factor of nine to more than $117 billion – nearly ten times more than the amount spent on tickets to the movies!

AN EASY WAY TO STOP GAMBLING

I was a confirmed nicotine addict, choking my way through 100 cigarettes a day and resigned to an early death. I was under the misapprehension that smoking was a habit I had acquired and lacked the willpower to quit. My revelation came when I realised that smoking was an addiction.

In that moment the fog lifted from my mind and I saw with extraordinary clarity that the problem was neither some weakness in my character, nor some magical quality in the cigarette.

Once I understood how the addiction worked, it was clear to me that smoking provided no genuine pleasure or crutch and, therefore, that stopping involved no sacrifice or deprivation. I quit there and then and started my mission to help the world's smokers do the same.

I called the method Easyway. It requires no willpower, no substitutes, no gimmicks, no nicotine products. It simply enables smokers to become happy non-smokers by unravelling the brainwashing that convinces them that smoking is a pleasure or a crutch. Once the illusion that they're making a sacrifice by stopping has been removed, they find it easy to quit because they don't feel deprived and they're happy to be free. The fact that my book, *The Easy Way to Stop Smoking*, has sold over 12 million copies in more than 40 languages worldwide and my stop-smoking clinics span more than 50 countries – and

> *The best throw of the dice is to throw them away.*
> **English proverb**

that this has been achieved almost entirely by word of mouth recommendation – is testimony to the power of the method.

I realised this method would work for all addictions and it has already been successfully applied to alcohol, other drugs and over-eating. Now we are applying it to an addiction that can become life-threatening much faster than smoking, alcoholism, drug abuse or obesity.

> *'But smoking, drug addiction, alcoholism and over-eating are all conditions of the body. Gambling doesn't affect the body.'*

In fact, all addictions are mainly a condition of the mind.

It's precisely because gambling does NOT appear to affect us physically that its ill effects are able to take hold so quickly. With smoking, alcohol, other drugs and junk food, there's a physical intolerance that must be overcome as our bodies try to protect themselves by rejecting the toxins.

Gradually, our tolerance level rises, we become better able to withstand bigger doses of the poison and our consumption increases accordingly, but it takes time. There's no physical barrier to the amount we can gamble. In other words, there's nothing to stop us going, in the space of a week, from a single ticket on the lottery to staking everything we own on a card game!

THE LACK OF A PHYSICAL ELEMENT IN THE WAY GAMBLING AFFLICTS US DOES NOT MAKE IT LESS OF A DANGER, BUT MORE OF ONE. IT ALSO MAKES THE ADDICTION EASIER TO HIDE

Easyway is about unravelling the misconceptions that drive you to do something that makes you unhappy, believing it will give you pleasure. This principle applies to gambling just as it does to drug addiction.

If you can see the mistake a heroin addict is making in thinking the next fix will solve his problem, you're already on the way to solving your own.

WHAT THIS BOOK WILL DO FOR YOU

Remember the claim I made at the start of this chapter:

This book will enable you to stop gambling immediately, painlessly and permanently, without the need for willpower or any feelings of deprivation or sacrifice.

Perhaps you're thinking, 'If it's that easy to quit gambling, why doesn't everyone do it?' The fact is that an increasing number of people are doing just that, by following this method. Regardless of how you feel about it right now, all I ask is that you set your preconceptions aside.

Believe me, Easyway works. Tens of millions of former addicts around the world can vouch for that. Many of them began thinking it sounded too good to be true but they put their trust in the method and followed it all the way to a successful conclusion. That's all I'm asking you to do: trust the method and you will discover that it works!

As you read through the book, I will give you a series of instructions. If you miss one of these instructions or fail to follow one, you will not be following the method. If you skip ahead and read the book in a different order, you will not be following the method.

Easyway is like the combination to a safe. I could give you all the numbers, but unless you apply them all in the correct order the lock will not spring open. In picking up this book and merely accepting the possibility that it might help, you have picked up the combination that will free you from the gambling trap. All you have to do is follow all the instructions.

THE FIRST INSTRUCTION
FOLLOW ALL THE INSTRUCTIONS

SUMMARY

- Whatever you've been told about problem gambling up until now has not worked for you.

- Gambling is an addiction.

- When you gamble you abandon control.

- You're not alone, although it may feel that way.

- Easyway works for all addictions.

- Quitting is easy if you know how.

- If you follow the instructions, you will succeed.

Chapter 2

WINNERS AND LOSERS

How do we first get the idea that gambling will make us happy?

You could argue that the first game of chance you ever play is life itself. The odds against your conception and birth are millions to one and, from the moment we come into the world, risk is ever present. In the playground, on the road, in the classroom, at home – we are surrounded by dangers which our parents warn us against.

As we grow older we learn that risk can be a game. We play dare, we push each other to take chances, we tease each other for being 'chicken'. The risk of being caught or hurt becomes a matter of honour. The game isn't much fun, in fact, but we play it to avoid losing face. And when we take a big risk and get away with it, we feel a buzz of elation that we perceive as a reward for our courage.

Parents and teachers may warn us about the danger of trying to take risks:

'Look before you leap.'

'Fools rush in where angels fear to tread.'

And yet, at the same time, we are fed messages that suggest the opposite:

'Nothing ventured, nothing gained.'

'Who dares wins.'

'Speculate to accumulate.'

From an early age we are given the impression that risk is a function of courage: the hero who risks all to save someone's life; the kid who does the most daring bike stunt; the businessman who invests everything he owns in one big idea. We admire these people and the way they're prepared to take risks. At the same time we tend to regard people who avoid risk as unadventurous or boring at best, cowardly at worst.

It's fixed in our minds that risk is something to be accepted, not avoided. And so, when it comes to gambling, it's like a gauntlet being thrown down: 'Are you big enough to take this on? Have you got what it takes?'

THE WILL TO WIN

At the same time as we are learning about risk, we are also learning about competition and games, about winning and losing. If we're taught well we learn how to lose gracefully and we also learn the thrill and sense of power that comes with winning.

Now the two come together. We already know how it feels to take a risk and get away with it. The feeling of euphoria is the same as the feeling we get when we win at games. We feel strong, clever, invincible. At the opposite extreme, losing can make us feel weak, stupid, worthless.

In addition, we are conditioned to regard money as a symbol of success. In other words, people with money are winners, those without are losers. It's another myth that disregards the fact that many rich people are miserable and many poor people are happy.

If you regard money as a symbol of success, you'll forever be chasing an illusion. The only true gauge of success is happiness. Happiness is the sign that everything in your life is as it should be. It's not measured in pounds or dollars or any other man-made currency. Happiness is our in-built indicator of when we've got our life in balance. The aim of this book is to help you to reach a point where you're truly happy.

In making a connection between risk and money and winning and success, we lay ourselves open to another harmful illusion: that when we take a risk and win, it's a reflection of our intelligence and skill.

IT'S FUNNY, ISN'T IT, THAT WHEN WE LOSE WE CURSE OUR LUCK, YET WHEN WE WIN WE COMMEND OURSELVES ON OUR SKILL AND JUDGEMENT?

As every loser knows, gambling isn't a matter of skill, it's a matter of chance. Therefore, when we win, it's not down to our skill and judgement, it's down to chance; nothing more, nothing less.

Sure, we may be able to improve our chances with a little more knowledge and understanding of the game and, in certain cases, the people we're playing against, but we are still reliant on Lady Luck smiling on us.

And yet, when we experience those first wins as gamblers, we feel that we have 'beaten the odds'. Winning makes us feel good about ourselves. We feel that sense of euphoria and equate it to winning a game of skill. In short, we kid ourselves that we have taken control.

IN HIS OWN WORDS: MICHAEL

I got into dog racing when I was about 13. I used to go with a friend and his dad and only put on small bets, but if you had a particularly good night you could win a tidy sum of money. I remember coming away with £50 once and I got a real buzz from making this money so quickly from such a small stake. It seemed so easy, I couldn't wait to go again.

Over the next few years I must have lost considerably more than I won, but I got a job as soon as I left school so I could afford it. The thing was, because I'd had those easy wins, I kept telling myself that the next big one was just around the corner. I convinced myself that I knew what I was doing.

When I couldn't get the satisfaction I wanted from the dogs, I turned my attention to other forms of gambling and started playing the machines in pubs. I reckoned all I had to do was wait until a machine hadn't paid out for a while, then move in to clean up.

I went from pub to pub, having some success, but then

I hit a run where I just couldn't seem to win. Whereas initially I would win a bit and walk away, now I wanted to stay in for the big payout. And of course, most of the time I lost.

I should have stopped right there, but I was hooked. I knew I *could* win, and the fact that I *wasn't* winning was like a red rag to a bull. I just kept charging back in again. Almost without realising it, I had got myself £5,000 in debt.

One of the things that non-gamblers find hardest to understand about gambling addicts is that, even after they have spent hours losing money, they still believe they're in control. Michael's addiction was slot machines. When he was at his worst he would spend hours at a time pumping coins into the slots, one after the other, non-stop. He wouldn't stop for a drink, he wouldn't stop to go to the bathroom. Why? 'I felt the machine would start paying out any minute.'

In other words, he believed he'd got the machine to a point where it was bound to pay him back everything he'd put in and more, and if he walked away, even for a minute, he would lose control of that situation.

Of course, he kept pumping money in and, more often than not, the big pay-out never came.

Winning is the worst thing that could happen to the novice gambler. If it was nothing but losing, it would be easy to recognise that it's a futile battle against unfair odds, and walk away to find a better way to spend your time and money.

But winning changes everything. The fact that we know we can win because we have already done so gives us the argument we need to keep gambling, even when we sense we're out of our depth.

Consider the following:

1. If we never won, we would not gamble.

2. If it were possible to win all the time, no one would want to stop and you would not be reading this book.

3. Gambling leads to debts/losses because the odds are stacked against us.

4. Winning is the lure in gambling, but since we don't actually win overall – we lose – it's an illusion

5. Every time we win, it makes winning seem more possible in future. Every time we lose, it makes gambling seem more necessary to cover our losses.

6. The grandmother in Dostoevsky's *The Gambler* became addicted because her first bet was spectacularly successful. She knew winning was possible as it had happened to

her. Later when she returned to the tables to repeat her experience, she lost her entire fortune.

The will to win is what drives us to gamble in the first place, but it's not what keeps us hooked. I will come to that soon, but first let's examine the belief that we can beat the odds.

AN EASY WAY TO LOSE

According to the old saying, a fool and his money are soon parted. That might suggest that all gambling addicts are fools. But the fact is that many highly intelligent people have found themselves trapped in gambling addiction and powerless to reason their way out of it.

They're not fools, but they have been trapped by a giant industry that profits from spreading the illusion that gambling is simply harmless fun, when in reality it's the fastest-growing addiction of the 21st century.

It's easier to gamble today than at any other time in history. The internet has opened up countless new ways to lose your money, as well as bringing traditional casino games right into our homes. We don't need to dress up in a tuxedo and go into town to play roulette any more, we can do it without even having to get out of bed!

All the hurdles that may once have made us stop and think twice about gambling have been removed. Switch on the TV and you'll find a government-endorsed programme actively encouraging you to participate in the national lottery. Change channel and you find a game show in which contestants are encouraged to gamble. These days it seems virtually every other advert on TV is for some form of gambling and the same images are now being used to sell the illusion as were previously used to sell alcohol and nicotine – sexy, alluring, aspirational.

> *Gambling is the son of avarice and the father of despair.*
>
> **French proverb**

Governments have eased legislation, allowing the gambling industry, or 'Big Gambling' as I call it, much more freedom in the way it goes about luring us in. The message is loud and clear: 'Gambling is ok.' It's no wonder that more people than ever before are falling into the misery of gambling addiction. As I said earlier, gambling is a matter of chance. Yet Big Gambling is constantly seeking ways to reinforce the belief that it's a matter of skill and judgement.

One example is the money quiz, such as the internationally successful *Who Wants To Be A Millionaire?* By asking questions of increasing difficulty in return for larger and larger winnings, the game creates a model whereby the more knowledgeable you are, the more you're likely to win. Again, there's the connection between winning and personal skill.

But the truth lies in one of the show's catchphrases: 'It's easy when you know the answer.' In other words, you'll only look in control and win if the question you're asked is one to which you happen to know the answer. And that's often purely a matter of luck. While the more knowledgeable contestants can be expected to progress further through the early rounds, there always comes a point where they have to make a decision: do I gamble on a hunch or do I walk away?

Those who walk away are made to wonder what might have been had they gambled. Those who gamble and lose are left feeling disappointed. Those who gamble and win go away feeling very pleased with themselves.

Because the gamble has been dressed up as a test of knowledge, we don't simply regard the winners as lucky and the losers as unlucky: we regard them as knowledgeable or ignorant.

In fact, the clever people are those running the game, because they're the ones in control.

LAME EXCUSES

Despite all the changes in gambling legislation and the many new ways to gamble, one time-honoured rule remains true:

THOSE WHO SET THE ODDS ALWAYS WIN IN THE END

Every gambler knows this, and yet we continue to believe that we can buck the trend. It's just one of the many delusions that keep gamblers trapped in their addiction.

Another is the delusion that gambling is pleasurable. Just as smokers delude themselves that they smoke because it gives them pleasure, rather than because they're addicted to nicotine, gamblers delude themselves that they gamble because they enjoy it.

But try asking them what exactly they enjoy about it and they will struggle for a convincing answer. Instead their reaction tends to be defensive and negative.

'It's a free country.'

'Life is short.'

'I've got it under control.'

'There are worse things in life.'

That's a strange way to talk about something that gives you pleasure. I get a great deal of pleasure from playing golf, but if I was asked why I play so often I would describe all the positives: the fresh air, the exercise, a sociable day out with friends, the challenge, etc. I wouldn't say, 'It's a free country.'

WHEN SOMETHING GIVES YOU GENUINE PLEASURE, YOU'RE ONLY TOO KEEN TO ENTHUSE ABOUT IT. YOU DON'T MAKE EXCUSES FOR WHY YOU DON'T STOP DOING IT!

In fact, gamblers, if they are truly going to be honest, sense that it's not really pleasure that keeps them gambling.

They may deny it or they may not understand it, but the real reason is that they have an addiction. The addiction is caused by illusions. In order to cure the addiction we must first remove the illusions.

Before we tackle the illusions that have led to your gambling addiction, it's essential that you realise you have an addiction and understand how you've been trapped.

SUMMARY

- Winning does not make you happy.
- Money is not a gauge of success.
- You cannot control the element of chance.
- The house always wins.
- True pleasures do not need excuses.

Chapter 3

WHY YOU ARE READING THIS BOOK

If we want to stop gambling, why can't we just go ahead and do so?

People with a gambling problem know that they must quit in order to get their life back under control. So why do they go on gambling?

The reason lies in the way our brains work. While our rational mind may tell us that gambling is causing us great harm and that we must stop, we continue to harbour an emotional desire to gamble. Why? Because we have been conditioned to believe that gambling gives us pleasure.

In order to break free from gambling addiction and allow our rational mind to regain control, we must undo the brainwashing that feeds the desire to gamble. In order to begin this process, first we have to recognise and accept that we have been brainwashed and take a positive attitude to escaping from the trap. It's a simple process but addicts tend to go about it the wrong way and that's why many find it difficult or impossible to escape.

In Chapter One I explained why I call my method Easyway: because it provides smokers with an easy way to quit. The same method has made it easy for alcoholics to quit drinking, for other drug addicts to stop taking drugs, for people with weight problems to stop over-eating and for people with debt problems to get out of the red. Now it will make it easy for you to stop gambling.

One of the differences between Easyway and other methods that claim to help overcome addiction is that other methods begin with the message that it's going to be difficult. This is a misconception that in itself keeps addicts in the trap, because the harder you think quitting is going to be, the more fearful you'll be of trying and the more you'll seek refuge in your addiction.

IT IS THE BELIEF THAT QUITTING WILL BE HARD THAT KEEPS GAMBLERS IN THE GAMBLING TRAP, DESPITE KNOWING THAT IT IS DESTROYING THEIR LIFE

Let's examine the reasons why you believe that quitting will be hard.

You probably know of other gamblers, or people with other addictions such as smoking, alcoholism or over-eating, who have tried to quit but failed. Perhaps you have tried yourself but found yourself pulled back into the trap by a force that was too strong for you to resist.

Every failed attempt to quit an addiction is incredibly damaging. Your self-esteem, which is already low because of the helplessness you feel as an addict, takes a further battering. You see your failure as a reflection on yourself and regard yourself as hopeless, weak and inferior to all those people who appear to sail through life without such problems.

At the same time, you confirm your belief that your addiction is a prison from which you'll never have the strength to escape.

And it's not only the person who tries and fails to quit who is affected by each failure. Every time we hear of someone else who has made a failed attempt to stop, it reinforces our belief that it must be difficult. But when we look at these people, and even when we look at ourselves, we see people who are, in many ways, strong.

People don't become addicts because they're weak or stupid. Many highly intelligent, strong people suffer the misery of addiction and find it impossible to escape. The reason they find it so hard is simply because they go about it the wrong way.

I MUST BE WEAK-WILLED

I said at the beginning of this chapter that in order to overcome gambling addiction you must take a positive attitude. You may have interpreted that to mean that you need to be strong-willed. No, not at all.

You only need willpower if you have a conflict of will, a tug-of-war of fear, going on in your mind. One part of your brain wants to stop since gambling is ruining your life; the other part wants to continue since it's afraid of losing a pleasure or crutch. Easyway removes the desire to gamble and the fear of stopping by changing the way you think about gambling, so that one side of the tug-of-war disappears, the conflict is resolved and you find it easy to quit.

I shall explain this in greater detail later, but I want you to get it clearly into your mind now that you do not need willpower to succeed.

People who try to stop gambling and fail assume that they lack the willpower to resist the temptation to gamble. They believe that it must be some weakness on their part that prevents them from escaping permanently. This is another misconception.

Furthermore, it's a misconception spread not only by the people who have a vested interest in our remaining hooked, but also by so-called 'help' organisations that aim to assist us in quitting. Easyway is the one method that does not rely on willpower. It also happens to be the most effective method the world has ever seen.

I said that this book will help you to solve your gambling problem painlessly and easily. When you reach the end and experience the elation of being free, you'll know exactly what I mean. Right now you may find it hard to believe that it's possible to succeed without suffering a period of deprivation and relying on willpower. **I ASSURE YOU: IT IS.**

For now, it doesn't matter whether you believe me or not. What is essential is that you accept that what I say *could* be true. What's the alternative? You know that the willpower method doesn't work. If it did, you wouldn't be reading this book.

You have a choice: you can choose to keep reading, follow the instructions and see if I'm right, or you can choose to continue the way you're going now, suffering the misery of gambling addiction, sliding deeper and deeper into the trap, losing money, friends, possessions and self-respect and coming ever closer to the point where you can see absolutely no way of going on.

If you think you've failed to quit in the past because you lack the willpower, I have nothing but good news. You don't need willpower. You failed because you were using a method that does not work. By picking up this book, you have embarked on a method that has been proven to work by millions of people all over the world. What's more, it makes it easy. All you have to do is keep reading and follow all the instructions.

DO I REALLY WANT TO QUIT?

In addition to the illusion that stopping gambling will be hard, some people believe that by stopping they will lose a valuable part of their identity. This shows how addiction can twist our judgement. Despite the misery, the torment, the loss of self-respect and all the other damaging effects of gambling, some gamblers continue to see their gambling problem as making them in some way daring and attractive.

There are a number of words in our language that have taken on meanings that are completely at odds with their original definition. 'Wicked' is a prime example, now commonly used to mean 'very good'. 'Safe' and 'dangerous' are two more. 'Safe' is a word that has essentially positive connotations, 'dangerous' is negative, yet when we apply these adjectives to people, those connotations can be reversed.

Someone who's safe is a bit boring, unadventurous, unlikely to surprise or entertain. By the same token, someone who's dangerous is exciting, unpredictable, never dull.

This twisted logic is often applied to characters in films and on TV. We tend to feel intimidated by people who show no vulnerability and we warm to the flaws in others. The shambolic character who battles through life against his own demons, be they drugs, gambling or whatever, usually wins our sympathy and affection over the one who appears to be in complete control and never puts a foot wrong.

We are fed these stereotypes time and time again, so it's hardly surprising that our own self-image often appears more attractive if there are obvious flaws.

If we take the gambling problem out of our life, maybe we will lose our shambolic charisma.

But wait a minute. Isn't it the case that you spend most of your time trying to conceal the fact that you have a gambling problem? If your flaws are so charming, why cover them up? Why not flaunt them for the world to see?

Of course, the reason we don't do that is because we are ashamed of the way gambling affects us. We don't want everybody to know that we have lost control, and that we're stuck in a trap from which we feel there's no escape.

DENIAL

All problem gamblers wish they could quit. The fact that they find themselves incapable of doing so makes them feel foolish and weak, and so they try to make themselves feel better by concocting excuses for why they continue to gamble.

'It's a bit of harmless fun.'

'I have a stressful job; gambling is my escape.'

'I can't play sport any more, so I gamble instead.'

These are all examples of how gamblers delude themselves. All gambling addicts know that it's not harmless fun. You know it too, that's why you're reading this book.

GAMBLING DOES NOT PROVIDE AN ESCAPE FROM STRESS, IT CREATES STRESS

If you feel stressed at work, you can guarantee that your stress will feel worse because of your gambling.

Sport and gambling are closely associated and some people who can no longer play sport turn to gambling to fill the void. But gambling does not replace any of the advantages of sport. It's not healthy, nor is it fair. You have no control over the outcome and the odds are stacked against you. Sport leaves you feeling good, even when you lose. It gives you a healthy sense of reward. Gambling never leaves you fulfilled. It creates a false hunger which makes you keep coming back for more, in the hope of attaining fulfilment. But you never will.

GAMBLERS MAKE UP EXCUSES FOR WHY THEY GAMBLE BECAUSE THEY'RE AFRAID TO ACCEPT THE REAL REASON: THEY'RE HOOKED

The reason gamblers deny this is because they're afraid of the consequences. If they acknowledge that they have an addiction, they will feel they should do something about it and they think that will be a difficult, painful process. Faced with that prospect, the familiarity of the gambling trap seems the lesser of two evils. Remember, overcoming your addiction with Easyway will neither be hard, nor painful. Remaining in the trap, however, will be both those things and worse.

THE ILL EFFECTS OF GAMBLING

I'm not going to lecture you on how gambling can ruin your life. Since you're reading this book, I assume you already know that. But it will help you also to be aware of some of the broader facts. Millions of people around the world are addicted to gambling and the number is rising steadily. The rise is particularly steep among groups that traditionally have not had easy access to gambling environments, such as women and young people. The internet has changed all that and, as a result, more and more people in all walks of life are suffering the misery of gambling addiction.

The total amount staked on gambling each year in the US is close to $100 billion and individual problem gamblers are running up lifetime debts in excess of $55,000 on average! The friend I referred to earlier accumulated more than £100,000 of debt in the UK by the age of 35! The stress this puts on relationships and individual happiness is unsustainable. The divorce rate among problem gamblers is twice that among non-gamblers and the suicide rate is twenty times higher. Two-thirds of problem gamblers turn to crime.

IN HIS OWN WORDS: KARL

I started gambling when I was less than 10 years old. My first bet was on the Grand National – my dad put it on for me – and my horse won. From that moment I was hooked.

I never saw it as a problem but I would take every opportunity to put money on a horse or a game. It wasn't that often because I didn't have much money but anything I earned or was given for birthdays or Christmas would usually go on gambling.

When I was 16 I got my own computer and that's when things started to get really bad. Very quickly I found I was spending time every day on internet sites, betting on everything from football to poker. I would lie to my parents to cover up what I was doing. I started pretending to be ill so I could miss school and spend the day on gambling sites. I'd been a good tennis player but I gave up playing because it was taking up too much time that I wanted to spend gambling. Gambling took over my life.

Whenever my parents showed concern I snapped at them and told them to get a life. I felt ashamed by my behaviour but I couldn't bring myself to open up to them. I had too much to lose. The worst thing was I was stealing from them. I had opened my online account with my dad's credit card. I still remember how I felt when

I was keying in the numbers on that card – a mixture of uncontrollable excitement and extreme shame and sadness. I felt like I was betraying my own parents for gambling, but I couldn't stop myself. It was horrible.

You might think they should have known what was going on, but I was brilliant at concealing it. I always made sure I covered my tracks, but I knew there'd come a day when my dad would check his credit card statement and see how much I'd cost him.

That day couldn't have come too soon. Being discovered was the best thing that ever happened to me. When my dad burst into my room brandishing the statement, I was sitting there with a bottle of pills in my hand, about to swallow the lot. I had hit rock bottom. I had gone from being a healthy, happy, sporty, intelligent lad to a miserable, short-tempered, sick, frightened individual, about to fail all my exams.

To be honest, I don't think I intended to take my own life. I wanted to be found out and that was the only way I could think of making it happen. Fortunately, my dad found out first.

There are aspects of Karl's story that will ring true for all problem gamblers. The obsession, the deceit, the short temper, the shame, the feeling of invincibility followed by the loss of control, the determination to try to solve the problem yourself through continued gambling, the underlying yearning to be rescued and, ultimately, the despair.

This is the true picture of what it's like when you're in the gambling trap. There's nothing romantic or charming about it. By choosing to persist with a life of gambling, you choose a lifetime of mental and physical anguish.

> *Luck sometimes visits a fool, but it never sits down with him.*
> **German proverb**

WOULDN'T YOU RATHER JUST WALK OUT OF THE TRAP, EASILY AND PAINLESSLY?

I promise you it can be done. Even if you still find that hard to believe, you might as well keep an open mind, follow the instructions and see for yourself. After all, you know the horror of the alternative.

YOU NEED TO REALISE THAT GAMBLING CONTROLS YOU, NOT VICE VERSA

WHY QUITTING IS EASY

We've established how you'll feel if you continue to gamble. Now let's contemplate the life that awaits you as a happy non-gambler.

Time

When you no longer spend your life seeking opportunities to gamble, you'll find you have so much more time to pursue the things you truly enjoy, like spending time with your family and friends, or just relaxing.

Honesty

You'll no longer feel the need to cover your tracks, conceal what you're up to, lie to your loved ones or steal to fund your addiction. As a result you'll feel far less stressed and defensive.

Self-respect

The realisation that you're no longer a slave to gambling will make you feel much better about yourself. Every time you think about your achievement in escaping the gambling trap, you'll feel a burst of elation and pride.

Control

With your life back under your control, you'll be able to make plans that will leave you feeling genuinely happy and fulfilled. You'll be in control of your time, your money, your behaviour and your destiny.

Health

Gambling affects your health in many ways, from the stress it causes through fear, deceit and anger to the physical harm you subject yourself to by becoming run-down and not eating properly.

When you're free of the gambling trap, you'll feel a fantastic glow of health and happiness.

All these wonderful benefits and many more await you when you walk free. In order to do that, you neither need willpower, nor to go through any transitional period of stress or deprivation. All you need to do is unravel the illusions that have kept you in the trap until now.

How do you know that what I say is true and what you've heard before is mere brainwashing? I promise you I will make that clear; for now I ask you only to accept that what I say could be true.

THE SECOND INSTRUCTION
KEEP AN OPEN MIND

You may regard yourself as an open-minded person, but in fact we go through life with our minds largely already made up about most things. For example, when you see the sun rise in the morning, you interpret it as a ball of fiery gases burning millions of miles away, which has the appearance of rising in the sky because the Earth is spinning. How do you know that's the case? Because you've been presented with some very convincing arguments by people with expertise in that field, and the explanation tallies with what you see. Not so long ago, people believed that it was actually a god driving a fiery chariot across the sky. That was the explanation put forward by the learned men of the time and it tallied with what people saw.

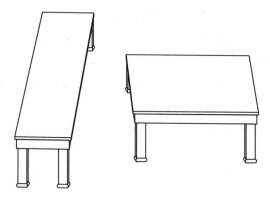

Now look at the two tables above. If I were to tell you that the dimensions of the rectangular table and the square table are exactly the same, would you believe me? I think not. You've already accepted that it's one square table and one rectangular one because that's what I've told you it is and it tallies with what you see. However, I assure you they're both identical. Take a ruler and measure them. Extraordinary, isn't it! What this shows is that our minds can be easily tricked into accepting as true something that is false.

WHEN YOU STARTED GAMBLING YOU BELIEVED THAT YOU WERE DOING SO OF YOUR OWN FREE WILL, BUT WHAT IF YOU WERE BASING YOUR CHOICE ON FALSE INFORMATION?

This is why I want you to remember the diagram of the tables and keep an open mind, so that even if I tell you something that you find difficult to believe, you'll accept the possibility that what I say is true.

SUMMARY

- We are brainwashed into believing that gambling gives us pleasure.

- Failing to quit by using willpower reinforces the belief that it's hard.

- You do not need willpower to succeed.

- There's nothing charming about a problem gambler.

- Addicts lie to themselves to cover up the real reason why they gamble.

- Gambling controls you, not vice versa.

- The second instruction: keep an open mind.

Chapter 4

FIRST STEPS TO FREEDOM

IN THIS CHAPTER
•HOW EASYWAY WORKS
•GETTING FREE AND STAYING FREE
•SEEING ADDICTION FOR WHAT IT IS

Your escape from the gambling trap has already begun!
Our job now is to remove your desire to gamble.

I'm sure by now you're eager to discover the secret of this solution to your gambling problem and you're probably wondering why I don't just tell you the magic formula without further ado. I must make two things clear:

1. It is not a secret.

2. There is no magic.

Easyway is a method that works by applying undisputable logic to strip away the brainwashing and replace it with rational thought, thereby removing your desire to gamble. The key consists of following the arguments and the instructions I give you while you read the book and it must be used like the combination lock of a safe. Each step must be understood and applied in the correct order for the combination to work.

I have already given you the first two instructions and you're well on the way to freedom, but please be patient. The key to your escape does not lie in the final chapter or the first chapter, or any single chapter alone; the whole book is the key and you're already starting to use it.

The key works by removing your desire to gamble, because when you have no desire to do something, it requires no willpower to stop. In order to do that, we need to change your frame of mind. So let's identify what's wrong with your current frame of mind as a gambler, remove that from your way of thinking and let logic and reason undo the brainwashing you've been subjected to ever since you were a child.

> **MANTRAP!**
> A gambling addict is caught in a trap, just like someone who's walked into a mantrap. Between us we have the two ingredients that will set him free: he contributes a strong desire to be released and I have the key that will release him. All he has to do is follow my instructions.
>
> However, once he is released there's another danger: the trap still exists and we have to ensure that he does not walk into it again.

FREEDOM FOREVER

People with addictions like gambling, smoking and over-eating, are notorious for stopping and starting again. So while helping you to escape from the trap is the first step; we also need to ensure you never get recaptured. We do this by making sure you understand the nature of the trap.

Unlike a mantrap, the gambling trap isn't physical but psychological. It exists only in the mind – an illusion conjured up by brainwashing. Like the table illusion in the last chapter, you have been fed a false view of reality, which has created the illusion that you get some pleasure or crutch from gambling and that quitting will involve pain and sacrifice. But once you can see through the confidence trick, you'll never fall for it again.

It's also worth bearing in mind that millions of people have lived their lives without ever falling for the gambling trap despite being subjected to a massive amount of brainwashing.

This brings us to the real difference between the gambler and the non-gambler. Obviously one gambles and the other doesn't, but that isn't the whole story.

The crucial difference between gamblers and non-gamblers is that the latter never have the desire to gamble.

EASYWAY ENSURES THAT YOU ESCAPE
FROM THE TRAP PERMANENTLY BY
REMOVING YOUR DESIRE TO GAMBLE

Those millions of non-gamblers who live their lives without ever falling for the gambling trap are subjected to the same brainwashing as you and I; therefore, somewhere in their minds they will believe that there's some benefit to be enjoyed from gambling. They, like you, are also aware of the misery that gambling can cause and they're able to rationalise that there's no sense in inflicting that on themselves. They're able to maintain the power of reason over temptation because, luckily for them, their reasoning has not been affected by addiction.

EASYWAY DOES NOT REQUIRE THE POWER OF REASON TO OUTWEIGH TEMPTATION; IT REMOVES TEMPTATION ALTOGETHER

No one forces you to gamble. You do so yourself. The fact that part of your brain wishes you didn't, or can't understand why you do, doesn't change the situation.

As long as you retain the desire to gamble, you'll suffer a feeling of deprivation when you stop. You'll have to use willpower to fight this sense of deprivation and you'll remain at risk of walking back into the trap at any time.

Easyway permanently removes the desire to gamble so that you do not go through life feeling deprived or resentful, or having to resist temptation.

Do you think that sounds impossible? If you do, that's because of the distorted way you see gambling. Non-gamblers have no desire to gamble nor did you until you got hooked. There are also large numbers of ex-gamblers who once thought they could never get free from the trap but have now escaped.

Soon you will join them.

PRODUCT PROFILE

There are many harmful products in the world. See if you recognise this one from my description:

- **Highly addictive: hooks its victims quickly and in many cases they remain hooked for life.**

- **Very expensive: the average addict will spend around £50,000 in their lifetime.**

- **Pushers provide the first fix for free, then squeeze addicts for increasingly high payments.**

- **Pushers set the price, addicts are powerless to negotiate.**

- **The more miserable it makes you, the more helpless and dependent on it you feel.**

- **Side effects: stress, anxiety, poverty, depression, aggression, loss of self-esteem, loss of focus, dishonesty, shame, guilt, isolation and, in extreme cases, suicide.**

- **Advantages: none.**

It's not the most compelling product profile, is it? Why would anyone blow £50,000 to put themselves through all that? Yet it has millions of customers and more are signing up for it every day. You've guessed it, this is a description of gambling.

Anyone who reads this product profile in isolation, rather than within the pages of a book on gambling addiction, would probably assume it was a description of a class A drug, such as heroin. That's because we see heroin for the vile addictive poison it is, whereas we have a distorted view of gambling.

We need to rectify this, and to do that I need you to understand that the trap you're in as a gambler is very similar to that of a heroin addict. It's a mental trap, not a physical one, and all you need to do to escape is to change your frame of mind. But first it's essential to understand and accept that you're in a trap.

It's easy for us to recognise the heroin trap. The media portrayal of heroin is quite clear: ADDICTION! SLAVERY! POVERTY! MISERY! DEGRADATION! DEATH!

But the media portrayal of gambling is completely different. Happy, beautiful people, smiling, showing no signs of strain or anxiety, laughing all the while as the wheel spins or the numbers are drawn. The message is straightforward: 'Gambling makes you happy.'

As you read this book, we will remove these illusions from your mind so that, instead of seeing gambling as a pleasure or crutch, you'll see it as the destructive force it really is. By the time you finish the book, your frame of mind will be such that, whenever you think about gambling, instead of feeling deprived because you can no longer gamble, you'll feel overjoyed because you no longer have to.

SUMMARY

- The gambling trap exists only in the mind.
- In order to escape permanently you must remove the <u>desire</u> to gamble.
- Gambling addiction is very similar to drug addiction.
- Once you understand the trap, your desire to gamble will be removed and you will be free.

Chapter 5

THE TRAP

All addicts are caught in an ingenious trap. Whatever the addiction, the trap works in the same subtle and insidious way.

It's easy to understand how smoking is an addiction. Tobacco contains a drug called nicotine, which makes smokers feel uptight as it leaves the body. If smokers light a cigarette during this withdrawal period, they feel more relaxed as the withdrawal is partially relieved. Thus they're fooled into believing they get a genuine pleasure or boost from smoking. In fact, they're just trying to get rid of the empty, insecure feeling of the body withdrawing from nicotine, which non-smokers don't suffer anyway.

EACH CIGARETTE DOES NOTHING MORE THAN
MAKE THEM FEEL HOW A NON-SMOKER FEELS
ALL THE TIME

It seems reasonable to assume, therefore, that all you need to do to cure the addiction is to remove all the nicotine from the smoker's body. Nicotine is a fast-acting drug that quickly starts to pass out of the bloodstream and leaves the body completely within three days. Surely, then, a smoker only needs to survive without a cigarette for three days and the addiction will be cured?

But we all know this isn't the case. Smokers who try to stop by using willpower can go on craving cigarettes for weeks, months, even years after quitting. Some poor souls do so for the rest of their life. This is because they continue to suffer the illusion that smoking gave them a pleasure or crutch and so they feel deprived.

And this is the fundamental irony about addiction: the addict is deluded into thinking that salvation lies in the very thing that's causing the misery. The problem may be triggered by the chemical in the body, but it festers and grows in the brain.

I've explained how addicts are fooled into thinking that the temporary relief from withdrawal gives them a genuine high. The body's instinctive response to the stress, insecurity and anxiety of not knowing whether you will win or lose triggers the release of chemicals in the brain which alleviate that stress. As these chemicals then leave the brain, you experience an empty, insecure feeling. This is withdrawal. If you gamble again, the chemicals are released again which relieves the withdrawal and fools you into believing you are getting a genuine boost. In natural circumstances the release of these chemicals is triggered by such things as pleasure, pain, excitement and fear. But when triggered by gambling they are produced in much greater quantities than nature intended.

You might think this sounds great: surely the more of those chemicals you can produce, the better you'll feel? But it doesn't work like that. Think about a TV set. It requires electricity to function properly and it runs very happily on 240 volts. Send 10,000 volts through it, however, and you'll probably find it rapidly turns into a pile of molten plastic!

Fortunately, the human body is better designed to handle such overloads but the principle is the same: it only needs a limited amount of each chemical to create the desired effect. Flood your brain with an overdose of dopamine, say, and it will reprogramme itself by effectively building a buffer, so that next time it gets flooded the effect won't be so extreme. Therefore, it will take more of the chemical to have the same effect. This is known as building tolerance. Repeat the process over and over again and your brain will build an increasing tolerance, until it hardly responds to the chemical at all.

When the initial flood subsides and the brain adjusts to its normal levels, we are left feeling lower than before. This is what we call withdrawal. Most people associate withdrawal with an attempt to quit, but in fact we experience the symptoms of withdrawal between every 'fix'. It can best be described as a slight feeling of unease, like an itch that needs to be scratched. And so we scratch it – we gamble again and flood our brain with chemicals.

The chemicals partially relieve the withdrawal symptoms. I say partially because the tolerance built up means that, even while gambling, the withdrawal is never completely relieved. Nevertheless this creates creates an illusion of pleasure – like the relief you feel when you take off a pair of tight shoes at the end of the day. We mistake this illusion of pleasure for genuine pleasure and thus reinforce the false belief that gambling gives us some sort of pleasure or crutch.

Understanding this aspect of addiction enabled me to see that addicts aren't always addicted to an addictive substance, and so as well as applying Easyway to nicotine and other addictive drugs like alcohol, heroin and cocaine, I was able to apply the method to other addictions like over-eating and gambling.

There's no addictive substance required to lure victims into the gambling trap. Just as smokers are drawn to smoking by illusions of cool, sophisticated role models, gamblers are lured into gambling by similar role models and fantasies of winning and outsmarting everyone else. That is all it takes to start us gambling. Once we've started, it's the illusion of pleasure that hooks us.

Pleasure: true or false?

It's important to be clear about the difference between genuine pleasure and false pleasure. Pleasure and reward are vital to our survival. It is these emotions that we derive from sex and good food, for example, that ensure we continue to reproduce and eat healthily. These activities give us a genuine boost that lifts our mood above the norm. When the effect wears off, we are not left feeling low. Indeed, there is often a lingering satisfaction that can remain with us for life.

False pleasures leave no lingering satisfaction. On the contrary, they leave us feeling below par. The illusion of pleasure that they give us is nothing more than the partial alleviation of discomfort, like taking off tight shoes. Would you wear tight shoes all day, just for the 'pleasure' of taking them off?

Genuine pleasures leave us feeling happy. False pleasures leave us feeling empty. Many gamblers believe that gambling gives them pleasure, but I've yet to meet a gambler who claims it makes them happy. Happiness is the sure sign of genuine pleasure and your happiness is the ultimate aim of his book.

Remember this distinction as you read on. It will help you realise and accept that gambling gives you no genuine pleasure whatsoever.

FILLING A VOID

It's helpful at this stage to understand why we are drawn to things that we know to be a threat to our health and happiness. As children, with relatively little knowledge, we content ourselves with innocent games. As adults, with more knowledge, we lay ourselves open to more harmful pursuits. Why?

It's a paradox, which is caused by an emptiness that opens up during our development, starting from birth. I call it 'the void' and it affects all of us to different degrees.

The shock of birth leaves us desperately seeking security. We reach for our mothers and they protect us. Our neediness and vulnerability continues through childhood, when we're cocooned from the harsh realities of life in a fantasy world of make-believe.

Before long we discover that Santa Claus and fairies do not exist. At the same time we're forced from the safety of home, to school and a new set of fears and insecurities. We look more critically at our parents and it begins to dawn on us that they're not the unshakeable pillars of strength that we had always thought them to be. They have weaknesses, frailties and fears, just as we do.

The disillusionment leaves a void in our lives, which we tend to fill with pop stars, film stars, TV celebrities or sports personalities. We create our own fantasies. We make gods of these people and start to attribute to them qualities far in excess of those they possess. We try to bask in their reflected glory. Instead of being complete individuals in our own right, we become followers, impressionable fans, leaving ourselves wide open to suggestion.

In the face of all this bewilderment and instability, we look for support, for a little boost now and then. We instinctively look to our role models and, quite naturally, copy the things they appear to be doing for comfort and relaxation: drinking, smoking and gambling. But these things don't fill the void, they make it worse.

HOW THE TRAP WORKS

All addicts are caught in the same ingenious trap. When I describe how the trap works for gamblers, you'll see how this is the case. The trap is similar to a pitcher plant, which lures flies into its digestive chamber with the sweet smell of nectar. The plant is shaped like a funnel, the inside of which is coated in a sweet, slippery nectar and at the bottom is a pit containing liquid. The fly lands on the rim and begins to drink. As it does so it feels itself slipping down the funnel towards the pit, in which the drowned bodies of other flies are slowly being digested. But instead of flying away, the fly continues to drink. The nectar tastes good – it seems like the best thing in the world, but it's the very thing that is luring the fly to its death.

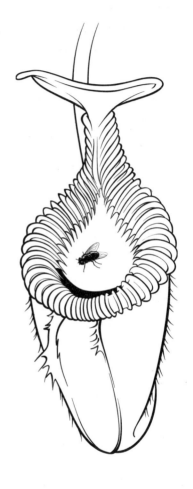

Just as the full horror of its predicament doesn't dawn on the fly until it's past the point of no return and it realises it can no longer escape, gamblers don't realise they're stuck in the trap until they're well and truly hooked. Indeed, many gamblers have lived and died without even realising that they're addicts. They believe that they're in control and gambling because they enjoy it. Only when gamblers try to escape do they realise they're in a trap.

Winning is the lure in gambling, just like the nectar in the pitcher plant, but since we lose more than we win, it's an illusion.

Before we gamble for the first time, we're aware of the arguments against it. We know that it's a slippery slope into destitution, that the chances of coming out on top are virtually nil and that it can become obsessive. We convince ourselves that for us it will be different – we'd never let it get to that stage. We might also be aware that it can sometimes lead us into contact with undesirable characters and possibly even turn us into undesirable characters ourselves. We also know that debts can mount up if they're not properly managed. In short, we know that gambling is something to be avoided.

Yet we also know that millions of people gamble every week without losing everything they love and possess. At the same time, the gambling industry bombards us with enticing ways to gamble.

£50 BONUS TO EVERY NEW PLAYER!

YOUR FIRST FIVE BETS FREE!

WIN WITH A LOSING HAND!

MONEY-BACK SPECIALS!

These messages are accompanied by images of smiling, happy people holding great wads of cash – people just like us. Or rather, just like we would like to be. And so we take the plunge and place our first bet. Despite our nervousness, nothing bad happens. In fact, it was fine. We might even have come out on top. Even if we didn't, we probably only gambled what we could afford to lose without it causing us any aggravation.

But it's not enough. Buoyed by our newfound confidence and the novelty of suddenly being 'a player', we decide to try another bet. We've already proved that we can handle it. After all, it's just a bit of harmless fun; we're not about to go headlong into debt, are we?

We're more confident than we were the first time, so we take it a bit further. We feel we're in control, but in fact gambling has already started to exert an insidious grip on our life which will become tighter and tighter. We begin to feel the need to gamble, as if something is missing when we can't do it. In fact, there is something missing: the chemical levels in the brain have been reset and we no longer derive satisfaction from normal, everyday pleasures.

> *It's very hard indeed to walk away from a winning streak, and even harder to leave the table when you're on a losing one.*
> **Cara and Ray Bertoia** *(authors)*

In the early days we're able to con ourselves that we remain in control of when and how much we gamble and that there will be no problems. However, as time goes on and the void created by gambling addiction grows, we begin to sense that we're slipping further and further into a dark pit. It's an unpleasant, insecure feeling that creates further anxiety and stress. Unfortunately, however, the only thing that seems to relieve the void is the placing of another bet. The addiction has taken hold.

Just as we reach for a pill to get rid of a headache, we reach for a temporary fix to take away this unpleasant feeling: we gamble again. Rather than dealing with the real cause of the problem, we use a temporary fix as an anaesthetic.

Like any anaesthetic, it soon wears off. Now, because the problem has not been addressed, the stress is worse than before. The need for a painkiller is intensified. We gamble again, raising the stakes, just as a drug addict increases the dose. The highs become more short-lived, the lows more intense and the net effect is an increasingly rapid descent in our level of wellbeing, like the fly sliding towards the bottom of the pitcher plant.

This is how the trap works. It's how all addictions work.

THE ADDICT SEEKS RELIEF IN THE VERY THING THAT IS CAUSING THE MISERY

NATURE'S WARNING LIGHT

The way we try to anaesthetise our pain is an example of how easy it is to fool our intellect. Say you have a toothache and reach for the painkillers. After a while the pain subsides and you feel better. But has the problem with your tooth gone away? Of course not. The pain has just been suppressed.

The pain was serving a useful purpose: it was telling your brain and body that there's a problem with your tooth, which needs sorting out. By suppressing the pain and dealing with the symptom rather than the cause, you prevent your body from responding to the problem appropriately. In the case of a toothache, the most appropriate response is to go to the dentist. Other ailments are often best healed by the body's own defence systems. By removing the symptom, you can undermine your body's ability to deploy these systems.

Imagine you're driving a car and the oil light comes on. What do you do? Remove the bulb from the warning indicator? Or pull over and top up the oil? Both actions will stop the oil light from flashing; only one will prevent the engine from seizing up.

AN INEVITABLE DECLINE

The nature of the trap is depicted by the diagram overleaf. It is a graphic illustration of a gambler's level of wellbeing in life. Remember, happiness is the sense of wellbeing that we get from genuine pleasures. such as playing games or being with friends. False pleasures erode your happiness and wellbeing. Before you start gambling you enjoy genuine pleasures that take your level of happiness above par. When the feeling subsides you return to par. Of course, there are genuine lows in life, too, which take you below par, and when you get through them you return to par.

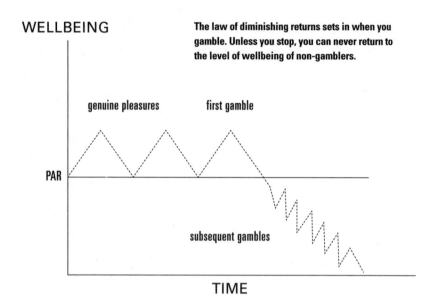

WELLBEING

The law of diminishing returns sets in when you gamble. Unless you stop, you can never return to the level of wellbeing of non-gamblers.

genuine pleasures   first gamble

PAR

subsequent gambles

TIME

When you hijack genuine pleasures by gambling, you mistakenly think the feeling of genuine pleasure created by watching or playing sport, or taking on challenges, is created by gambling. But this is an illusion. The chemicals released by gambling don't take you any higher, but the withdrawal from them takes you lower when they subside. Now your idea of par is lower than it was before as you feel the uneasy symptoms of withdrawal, like an itch you want to scratch. I call this withdrawal the Little Monster. It's so slight as to be almost imperceptible and it quickly passes. The Little Monster was created the first time you gambled and triggered the flood of chemicals. It feeds on those chemicals and, when you don't give it what it wants, it demands a fix. This too is barely perceptible, but the real problem is that it arouses another monster.

This second monster isn't physical but psychological. I

call it the Big Monster and it's created by a combination of the brainwashing that has led you to believe that gambling provides a pleasure or crutch and the physical addiction, i.e. the Little Monster. The Big Monster interprets the Little Monster's demands as 'I need to gamble', and so you end up trying to relieve a craving by doing the very thing that caused it in the first place.

So you scratch the itch – you gamble – and you experience the illusion of pleasure. But it doesn't give you the genuine high that you knew as a non-gambler; it gives the illusion of a high, which quickly wears off and the withdrawal takes you back down to a new low.

Perhaps you're thinking, 'So what? Won't the boost I get from gambling make me feel better, even if it's an illusion?' No, it won't! The reason you're reading this book is that gambling is ruining your life, taking your wellbeing lower and lower. As time passes, you slide further and further down the scale and feel worse and worse.

As the body builds tolerance to protect itself from the chemical overloads, the quantities of chemicals you produce naturally have a diminishing effect. That's why addictions leave you feeling dissatisfied and unstimulated, more stressed, less able to concentrate, tired, lethargic and miserable. The chemicals that normally keep these feelings in check are no longer having an effect.

Now you need a bigger 'fix' to get the chemicals to work. For the drug addict this means a bigger dose of the drug; for the gambler, it means raising the stakes.

The result is another false high and an ever lower low. No matter how big a 'fix' you give yourself, you can never return to par because of your body's increasing tolerance. As long as you keep relying on gambling to give you the illusion of pleasure, your wellbeing will continue to fall lower and lower.

At the same time, your physical and mental wellbeing are also continuously being damaged in other ways. You stop taking care of your physical health and you become more and more conscious of the miserable trap that has imprisoned you. This combination of factors means that as you go though life as a gambler, the lows get lower and the false high you come back to when you gamble goes down in proportion. By the time you're ready to accept that gambling is causing you nothing but harm, you're so far down in the trap that, like the fly in the pitcher plant, escape can seem impossible.

The good news is that when you quit with Easyway, escape is easy and, what's more, you can very quickly go back again to your original par – the genuine happiness of the non-gambler. Remember, millions of people, who've found themselves in the same trap and been convinced that they will never be able to escape, have got free and so will you.

Consider your losses as the equivalent of the unsightly fat on somebody who is overweight, or as the smoker's cough or the threat of lung cancer. You try to cover them up, you pretend they're not there, you kid yourself that they're under control; you'll deal with them soon, just not yet. But these are ever-increasing, dark shadows looming at the back of your mind and as you slide further and further into the gambling trap, they loom larger and larger, making you more and more miserable.

Like the fly, you only realise you're trapped by gambling long after you become hooked. But there's one crucial difference between the pitcher plant and the gambling trap:

IT'S NEVER TOO LATE TO ESCAPE FROM THE GAMBLING TRAP

Unlike the fly, you're not standing on a slippery slope. There's no physical force compelling you to gamble more. The trap is entirely in your mind. The fact that you are your own jailor is an ingenious aspect of the trap and fortunately for you it is also its fatal weakness. You have the power to escape by understanding the nature of the problem and following the simple instructions in this book.

WHAT'S STOPPING YOU FROM FLYING FREE?

When you see the gambling trap in these terms, the solution looks simple: stop gambling and just fly away. But as you know, when you're actually in the trap, nothing looks simple. That's because there are two major illusions clouding your judgement:

1. The myth that gambling gives you pleasure and/or a crutch.

2. The myth that escape will be hard and may be impossible.

You probably have good memories of certain times when you've gambled: perhaps a sweepstake in the office or a game of cards with your friends. But where did the real pleasure come from that day? Was it really the gambling that made your day? Or was it the company of your friends, the banter you had between you, the simple pleasure of playing a game with people you like?

Take away the gambling and the situation would still have been enjoyable. Take away the situation and the gambling would have not have given you any genuine pleasure.

As the fly is descending into the pitcher plant, there's a point at which it senses that all is not well and it thinks about flying off. For the fly, this point usually comes too late. It's physically stuck. For you there's no physical force preventing your escape and yet, when you sense that you're being consumed by gambling and want to get free, you feel you can't.

You know that the only way to free yourself from this misery is to stop and yet the thought of doing so is so daunting that you bury your head in the sand and keep sliding down into the pit.

In reality it's fear that keeps you hooked. The fear of being deprived of your pleasure or crutch, the fear that you've got to go through a period of deprivation and frustration to get free and the fear that maybe you'll never be completely free from the desire to gamble, and so will have to spend the rest of your life fighting the craving. You may have tried to stop before and failed because it was such a nightmare. But that's because you were using the wrong method.

You can make the simplest of tasks impossible if you go about it the wrong way. Try crossing a busy road drunk, with your eyes closed, and you're unlikely to make it. Do it in a more sensible way and nothing can prevent you from succeeding.

Get it clearly into your mind: you're not giving up anything. You're ridding yourself of a mortal enemy, which has been making your life miserable, damaging your wealth and health and threatening your very existence.

You have every reason to feel excited. By choosing to read this book, you've made it clear that you've reached the point in your descent into the gambling trap where you realise that you have a problem. Perhaps you reached that point a long time ago but didn't receive the correct instructions to help you escape.

Now you want to get free and start enjoying genuine pleasures again. This book is all you need to succeed. It's time to stop feeling miserable and start feeling excited about what you're about to achieve.

THE THIRD INSTRUCTION
START WITH A FEELING OF ELATION

From now on, I want you to put aside the idea that stopping will be difficult or traumatic. It's a myth. Instead, think about your escape as Nelson Mandela must have thought about his own after 27 years in prison. Think about the light, the freedom, the happiness. Think about your friends and family and how much life you have to share with them. Feel the excitement growing as that freedom draws nearer. Nothing stands in your way. Just make sure you understand the points I'm making and follow the instructions and your escape is guaranteed.

SUMMARY

- Addicts seek relief in the very thing that's causing the problem.

- An overload of brain chemicals does not give you an extra boost, but it does give you an extra low.

- The myth of pleasure and the belief that escape is hard keep you trapped.

- Gambling continually erodes your wellbeing.

- You're not giving up anything.

- The third instruction: start with a feeling of elation.

Chapter 6

ILLUSIONS

Gamblers believe they enjoy gambling. It's an illusion.

The belief that gambling gives you pleasure and that stopping is difficult are the two main illusions that prevent addicts from taking that easy walk out of the trap. Perhaps you're wondering how so many people could be taken in by these illusions and whether Easyway is simply a different form of brainwashing.

I admit, it seems extraordinary that the most sophisticated creatures on the planet should fall for illusions that cause them such damage. After all, are humans not the great survivors? We have devised ways to survive and thrive that have given us power over every other species on Earth.

The vital difference between human beings and wild animals is that animals survive almost entirely by instinct. We also use instinct to survive: it tells us when and what to eat, it alerts us to danger, it even helps us to find a suitable mate. But we have another tool, which has enabled us to rule over the animal kingdom: intellect.

Our intelligence has enabled us to learn and pass on our learning, with the result that we have developed into a highly sophisticated species that isn't only capable of building fantastic structures and machines, but also has an appreciation of art, music, romance, spirituality and so on.

Intelligence is a wonderful thing but it can go to your head; for it's our intelligence that has also led us astray. Instinct is nature's survival kit, but there are times when it conflicts with our intellect and when it does we tend to trust the latter.

For example, a sportsman needs a pain-killing injection in order to play. His instincts are giving the clear signal to rest and allow the injury to recover but his intellect tells him he can numb the pain and play on. The result is irreversible damage to his body. His instinct was right, yet he chose to side with his intellect.

Look again at the 'advances' mankind has made and you'll see that, rather than building on the advantages that nature has given us, we have devoted a remarkable amount of time and effort to self-destruction. I don't just mean the ever more sophisticated ways of killing each other in battle, but also the self-destruction caused by our eating habits.

How have we become a species of compulsive junk food consumers? By allowing our intelligence to trick our instincts. Refined sugar is a prime example. The reason we are so partial to refined sugar and all the sweets, cakes, drinks, etc., that contain it, is that it replicates the natural sugar in fruit. Nature designed us to eat fruit and our taste for its natural sugars is meant to keep us coming back for more. Refined sugar contains none of the goodness of fruit, yet it tricks our taste buds into thinking it's the same thing. Our intellect has enabled us to create a substance that fools us into thinking it's good when, in truth, it's extremely bad.

Our reliance on our intellect over and above our instincts lies behind most of the harm we do to ourselves as a species. It also explains why we take risks. After all, is risk not the intellectual choice to do something that we instinctively feel is a threat?

> *Remember this: The house doesn't beat the player. It just gives him the opportunity to beat himself.*
>
> **'Nick the Greek' Dandalos (gambler)**

As a species, we toy with our instincts for our own amusement. Fear is an instinct that triggers an adrenaline rush. This is designed to make us more alert and responsive when in danger and it's a feeling we call a 'buzz'. In order to get that buzz on demand, we deliberately put ourselves in the face of danger to trigger our own fear instinct. From playground stunts to bungee jumping, it is a facet of human nature to take risks in order to get a buzz. And the more we do it, the further we feel we have to push ourselves to get the same buzz. We have used our intellect to reprogramme our instincts.

Gambling is, by definition, just another form of risk. On the face of it, it seems much less risky than, say, parachuting, but we are still putting ourselves in the way of danger – the risk of losing. We now know that instincts are chemical responses in the brain. Gambling, like drugs, hijacks these response systems and creates false responses, such as false pleasure and reward, which the body mistakes for the real thing. The delusion is reinforced by misinformation.

In other words, if we are told that gambling gives us pleasure and at the same time we feel a mental boost when we gamble, it's easy to be convinced that this is the truth and push aside any conflicting suspicions we might have. It's when we make intellectual choices based on misinformation that our wellbeing begins to suffer. Wild animals do not experience bouts of self-loathing. Intelligence can create misery as well as happiness. The choice is ours. So why do we so often take the self-destructive path?

The reason is that we don't always realise we have an option. There are always people who stand to gain as a result of these destructive practices, be they arms dealers, drug cartels, the tobacco and alcoholic drinks industries, fast food chains, gambling firms or whatever, and they have become masters at exploiting our intellect to pass on false information and reprogramme our instincts.

Actually it's not intellect itself that is the flaw, it's the way we apply it. Our intellectual ability to communicate and absorb information is quite incredible. It has given us music, art, literature, sport and science – things that set us apart from all other creatures on Earth. Unfortunately, we are also able to communicate and absorb misinformation. Our intellect can easily be fooled.

Take a look at this jumble of shapes. What does it say to you?

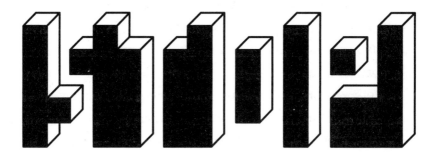

Is there a coherent message in it all? At first it can look like a random line of building blocks. There isn't really a meaningful message there at all, is there?

Now look again. This time, look at the shapes with your eyes half-closed and, by peering through your eyelashes, you can make a word appear. It might help if you move your head back a little (or to the side) and look at it from a distance.

Remember, you're not looking at the black type, you're looking at the white space between the type.

You should see the word STOP. Have you got it now? Obvious, isn't it? In fact, now that you can see it, I defy you to look at the same diagram and *not* see the word STOP. Now that you can see the pattern in the image, the truth should stay with you forever.

So why wasn't it obvious in the first place? Because we're programmed to look for information in the black type on a white page, and the thought of doing the opposite doesn't cross our mind. This is a graphic example of how easy it is to create confusion between your instinct and your intellect. The way gambling and other addictions work is to create a false sense of pleasure and reward, which your mind comes to mistake for the real thing. You have been conned into believing that you need to gamble in order to get a feeling of pleasure or support. As long as you continue to believe that, you'll remain in the trap.

I have explained how so many people get brainwashed in this way. Now you should also be able to see the answer to the second question:

HOW DO I KNOW THAT EASYWAY ISN'T JUST BRAINWASHING ME IN A DIFFERENT WAY?

When you see through an illusion and recognise the truth, you can never be fooled into seeing the illusion again. You fell into the gambling trap because you were under the illusion that gambling gave you pleasure and/or a crutch. And yet gambling has not made you happy or secure, it has made you miserable and insecure. The truth is there for all to see and, just like the STOP diagram, once you've seen it, nothing should be able to change your perception.

That's how you can tell the truth from the myths. Easyway isn't brainwashing, it's COUNTER-brainwashing. If brainwashing is the winding up of an elastic band around a pencil – making it tighter, and tighter, and tighter, fit to snap – then counter-brainwashing is the complete reverse – an unravelling, relaxing, calming, unwinding, harmless journey away from danger.

So let's take a closer look at the illusions.

I ENJOY GAMBLING

This is the most common excuse put forward by gamblers. 'Hey! It's just a bit of harmless fun.' We've established that it's anything but harmless, but let's put that aside for a moment and examine the argument that it's fun.

Have you ever studied yourself when you're gambling? I very much doubt that you have, but perhaps you have watched other gamblers from time to time. If so, you'll have noticed their deadpan look and the almost machine-like way in which they place their bets. They don't savour each bet they place. There's no sign of genuine pleasure each time they chance their arm on another throw of the dice, spin of the wheel or turn of the card. Each bet is swallowed up in the whole gambling experience.

I've explained how we build tolerance to the chemical overload caused by gambling and other addictions. This tolerance has the long-term effect of flattening out our emotions and desensitising us. We develop an indifference to losing and an indifference to winning. Therefore, the more we gamble, the more we suppress our ability to enjoy anything. One of America's biggest and most notorious gamblers stopped smoking at our New York clinic. He said his biggest win was $8 million in one night and his biggest loss $12 million. We asked him how it felt and he replied, 'On neither occasion did I feel anything.'

TAKE YOUR HEAD OUT OF THE SAND!

It's the addiction that fools gamblers that they get a genuine pleasure or crutch from gambling.

When they're not gambling they feel restless and uncomfortable, so they gamble and the uncomfortable feeling is temporarily relieved. It feels like a boost but it's only making them feel like a non-gambler feels all the time, since a non-gambler is not addicted and therefore does not suffer the restless, uncomfortable feeling of withdrawal in the first place. If you still have any doubts about this, review the diagram and explanatory text on page 82.

I LIKE THE RITUAL

Some gamblers claim they enjoy the ritual. By which they mean the dressing up, the journey to the casino or the races, the exchange of money for chips, the patter of the croupier, the cries of the bookies, the chalking up of the odds, etc.

Whatever arena you choose to gamble in, there's an abundance of ritual, all adding to the illusion of pleasure and excitement. But is the ritual really that enjoyable? We ritualise many things in life, but can you think of anything else we do purely for the pleasure of the ritual? If it's the ritual that's so pleasant, why don't we alter it ever so slightly by not actually placing any bets, thereby still retaining the pleasure of the ritual and at the same time avoiding the nasty part that we tend to overlook: the loss, the stress, the self-loathing, the slavery, the degradation? The fact is the ritual wouldn't be the same without the final act. It would be like dining out without the food.

Dining out involves a fairly elaborate ritual. We dress up, we are helped into our seats by the waiters, we unfold the napkin and place it in our lap, we peruse the menu, sample the wine and so on. It's all part of the pleasure of eating out. But imagine if you got to the part where everybody's getting their food and you got nothing. You ask the waiter what's happened to your order and he says, 'You've had the ritual, what more do you want?' Would you describe that as an enjoyable experience?

Any gamblers who say they do it for the ritual are kidding themselves. They do it because they're addicted to it, and so feel empty and uncomfortable when they're not doing it. Non-gamblers do not suffer this empty, uncomfortable feeling. Nor did you before you started gambling and the good news is nor will you once you've got free.

IT'S JUST A HABIT

The words 'habit' and 'addiction' are often used synonymously these days. People talk about a 'drug habit'. But there's a clear distinction between them and it's absolutely essential that you understand what it is, otherwise you won't fully grasp the nature of the trap.

With habits, you're in control. If you want to break a habit, it's easy. The important thing is the underlying reason why certain behaviour becomes habitual. That reason might be beneficial. If so, why break the habit? It's very unlikely anyone would deliberately repeat behaviour that provided them with no benefit whatsoever, unless, of course, they were deluded into believing that it was beneficial: as in the case of all addictions, including gambling.

Gamblers believe that they choose to gamble because they enjoy it. But if, at any time, they were to take their head out of the sand and list all the advantages and disadvantages of being a gambler, the conclusion would be, 'You're a mug. Stop doing it!' This is why all gamblers (and, incidentally, all other types of addicts) instinctively feel stupid.

> Gambling: The sure way of getting nothing from something.
>
> **Wilson Mizner (playwright)**

In fact, they're not stupid. There's a powerful force that more than balances the scales, and that force is called addiction. You don't need me to tell you this. The way gambling has been making you feel is proof enough already! Isn't it true, that a feeling has been nagging away at the back of your mind, that you're not doing this because you like it, or because you enjoy it, you're doing it because you're a junkie, seemingly compelled to carry on against your better judgement, never being allowed to stop?

By pretending that it's just habit that makes you feel compelled to gamble, what you're really saying is, 'I don't even begin to understand why I gamble. I don't believe that I get any genuine pleasure from it at all. It's just a habit I've got into and, providing I can survive long enough without a bet, time will solve the problem and my desire to gamble will eventually go.' But you would be deluding yourself.

The only way to escape from the gambling trap easily and permanently is to understand how it works and accept the fact that you get no genuine pleasure or benefit from gambling. Only then will you be free from the temptation to fall back in. I don't mean you'll be able to resist the temptation, I mean there will be no temptation. You will have no desire to gamble.

IT'S THE WAY I'M MADE

Perhaps you believe your gambling problem is part of your personality. Either you put your failed attempts to quit down to a weakness in your temperament – i.e. a lack of willpower – or to a predisposition to gamble, over which you have no control – i.e. an addictive personality.

Either excuse is a cop-out. What you're effectively saying is, 'I can't help it. It's something to do with my genetic make-up or my personality which is beyond my control.'

The problem is that the bulk of information we receive about addictions such as gambling, smoking and alcoholism suggests that you *do* need willpower to quit and that some people have an addictive personality which makes it harder.

The fact that this misinformation is spread by reputable organisations, which, I have no doubt, act purely out of good intentions, only adds to its potency. Why would organisations dedicated to helping people stop gambling put out misinformation that makes it more difficult to do so? The simple answer is because they too have been brainwashed.

I'll explain more about the illusions regarding the addictive personality later. For now, remember the STOP diagram.

Once you look at it in a different way and see the true message, you can never be fooled by the illusion again. I asked you to keep an open mind because the truth is often the complete opposite of what we assume.

The claim that your gambling problem is down to a flaw in your personality is a form of denial. Rather than accepting that you have an addiction and taking the necessary steps to overcome it, you can say, 'I have no choice, I can't help it.' But why would any gambler want to say that? Why would anyone who is suffering the misery and slavery of gambling addiction make an excuse that took away their option to walk free?

> There is a very easy way to return from a casino with a small fortune: go there with a large one.
> **Jack Yelton (football coach)**

Gamblers, like all addicts, lie. They lie to themselves and others in order to perpetuate the illusions that enable them to avoid facing the reality of their addiction. Why do they opt for lies and continued imprisonment?

The answer can be encapsulated in a single word, which lies at the root of all addictions and which we will explore in the next chapter:

FEAR

SUMMARY

- The reasons gamblers give for gambling are excuses.
- No gambler really enjoys gambling.
- Gambling isn't a habit, it's an addiction – they're different things.
- Having a gambling problem isn't a sign of being weak-willed.
- Quitting with Easyway does not require willpower.
- Fear keeps you hooked.

Chapter 7

REMOVING YOUR FEARS

Gamblers are caught in a tug-of-war of fears, which make the prospect of stopping scary. It's time to remove these fears.

Gamblers make excuses to go on gambling because they're afraid of quitting. They've been deluded into thinking that they derive some pleasure or crutch from gambling, and so they fear life without it. At the same time, they're aware of the harm they're inflicting on themselves and their loved ones and they're afraid of where it might end up.

This tug-of-war of fear is typical of addiction. You hear it in the things addicts say. On the one hand: 'It's destroying me, costing me a fortune and controlling my life.' On the other hand: 'It's my little prop or pleasure. How can I enjoy or cope with life without it?'

What they fail to understand is that all these fears are caused by their addiction. They didn't suffer them before they became addicted and they need never suffer them again once they've quit – provided they used the right method to become free.

Fear is both an instinctive and an intellectual response. Instinct drives us to fight or flight, alerting us to danger and making us wary in potentially dangerous situations. Therefore, fear is vital to our survival.

However, the things that make us fearful can be either real or imaginary. Our intellect has enabled us to learn about potential dangers and how to avoid them, so much so that we can fear dangers of which there's no present evidence.

The fears associated with losing your job, for example, are intellectual. We have learned about the possible consequences of finding ourselves unemployed – e.g. having no money, being forced to sell your possessions, sacrificing the pleasures and comforts that you enjoy now – and so we do everything in our power to safeguard our job and make ourselves indispensible, even when there's no present threat of losing it.

In this instance our intellect does us a good service. But what if our projected fears are based on false information? Say, for example, you read in a magazine that fruit causes cancer. You would probably avoid eating fruit. You would also worry about the damage already caused by all the fruit you have eaten in your life.

I have yet to hear anyone claim that fruit causes cancer, but it's typical of the sort of scare stories with which we are bombarded on a regular basis.

Some of them are based on sound evidence, others are nonsense. A few years ago, a British doctor misleadingly linked the increasing incidence of autism in the UK to the MMR vaccine, leading to mass outbreaks of measles after parents refused to have their children inoculated. As consumers, it's difficult for us to know what to believe and we end up spending a lot of our life worrying about things that will never happen, while being blasé about things that will.

Fear is the basis of all addictions: the fear that you'll be deprived of a genuine pleasure or crutch, the fear that you have to go through some terrible trauma to quit and the fear that perhaps you can never get completely free from the craving. What never dawns on the addict is that all these fears are caused by the addiction. Non-addicts do not suffer these fears and one of the great gains of becoming free is to rid yourself of them.

It's only through the ingenious con trick of addiction that we are fooled into believing that quitting involves making a sacrifice. It's ingenious because it works back to front. It's when you're not gambling that you suffer the empty, insecure feeling. When you gamble, you feel a small boost, which temporarily relieves the insecurity and thus your brain is fooled into believing that gambling provides you with a pleasure or crutch, while, in fact, it's gambling that created the insecurity in the first place. So gambling gets the credit for relieving the feeling but not the blame for causing it. The more you gamble, the more it drags you down and the more you feel in need of your illusory crutch.

This is why gamblers and other addicts are on a loser. When they're gambling they wish they didn't have to. It's only when they can't gamble that it appears so precious. They mope for something that doesn't exist, an illusion: something that appears to them to be a pleasure or crutch but in reality is the complete opposite.

ONCE YOU UNDERSTAND THE GAMBLING TRAP COMPLETELY, YOU'LL HAVE NO MORE NEED OR DESIRE TO GAMBLE

THE FEAR OF FAILURE

Being addicted to gambling is like being in prison. Every aspect of your life is controlled by gambling: your daily routine, your hopes, your relationships, your financial situations, your view of the world, your suffering. Of course, you're not physically imprisoned. There are no walls or bars. The prison is in your mind. However, as long as you remain a slave to gambling, you'll experience the same psychological symptoms as an inmate in a physical prison.

If you've already tried and failed to quit gambling – or to break any other addiction – you'll know that it leaves you feeling more trapped than you did before. You've seen films where a prisoner is thrown into a cell and the first thing he does is run to the door and wrench at the handle. This confirms his predicament: he really is locked in.

Trying and failing to quit has the same effect on the addict. It reinforces the fear that there's no escape. This can be a crushing experience and many people conclude that the best way to avoid the misery of failure is to avoid trying to escape in the first place.

The twisted logic of addicts concludes that as long as they don't try to escape, they will avoid the possibility of failure.

The fear of failure is illogical. It's the fear of something that has already happened. The failure is the fact that they're addicts. As long as they remain addicts, they will remain failures. In the case of gambling, you suffer a compulsion to keep betting even though it's ruining your life and making you miserable. As long as that continues, you'll continue to feel a failure.

When channelled properly, the fear of failure can be a positive force. It's the emotion that focuses the mind of the runner on the starting blocks, the ballerina waiting in the wings and the student going into an exam. Fear of failure is the little voice in your head that reminds you to prepare thoroughly, to remember everything you've rehearsed and trained for and therefore to leave nothing to chance.

But the addict's fear of failure is based on an illusion. In fact, you have nothing to lose by trying, even if you fail. By not trying, you ensure that you remain permanently in the trap.

IF THE FEAR OF FAILURE PREVENTS YOU FROM MAKING THE ATTEMPT TO STOP YOU ARE GUARANTEED TO SUFFER THE VERY THING YOU FEAR

Moreover, the fear of failure isn't the only fear that keeps addicts imprisoned in the trap. There's also:

THE FEAR OF SUCCESS

It's a sad fact of the penal system that many long-term prisoners reoffend soon after they're released. This depressing phenomenon occurs not just because they haven't learnt the error of their ways, but because in some cases they actually *want* to go back inside. They yearn for the 'security' of the prison. Life on the outside is alien and frightening for them, more frightening than life on the inside. It's not what they know. They don't feel equipped to handle it.

The same fear afflicts some addicts. They're afraid that they won't be able to enjoy or cope with life without their 'crutch', that they'll have to go through some terrible trauma to get free and that they'll be condemned to a life of sacrifice and deprivation.

> *In gambling, the many must lose in order that the few may win.*
> **George Bernard Shaw**
> **(author)**

In the case of the person suffering from gambling addiction, failure means remaining in the old, familiar prison cell; success means coming out into the unknown and that can seem daunting. Like those long-term prisoners, you may be fearful of what life will be like outside and dread the self-discipline, sacrifice and deprivation that you fear will be your fate.

Perhaps you've been deluded into believing that life without gambling is boring. Though you're well aware of the misery that your gambling causes, you may also have come to think of it as part of your identity. Perhaps you even regard it with a perverse kind of respect, as if there were some sort of shambolic charisma about it. The image of the chain smoker, the heavy drinker and the gambler can suggest that it makes us attractive. Heroic characters in books and films are frequently portrayed as having one or more of these characteristics and the implication is that it makes them human, charming, exciting, attractive. To the audience maybe; in real life it makes them miserable and very difficult to live with.

REMOVING THE TUG-OF-WAR

Cast the illusions aside and be clear in your mind: the panic feeling that makes you afraid even to try to quit gambling is caused by gambling, not relieved by it. And one of the great benefits you'll receive when you get free is never to suffer it again. The tug-of-war of fear disappears when you quit because all the fears are caused by the same thing: gambling.

TAKE AWAY THE GAMBLING AND THE FEAR GOES TOO

Remember, you had no need to gamble before you started and you'll have no need to gamble once you've stopped. If I could transport you now into your mind and body at the time when you finish reading this book, you might ask, 'Will I really feel this good?' Fear will have been replaced by elation, despair by optimism, self-doubt by confidence, apathy by dynamism. As a result of these psychological turnarounds, your physical health will improve too. You'll enjoy a newfound energy, as well as the ability truly to relax.

Maybe you've tried to stop in the past and gone for weeks, months, even years without gambling, but still found that you missed it. Trust me, this method is different. You will not miss it. You are not giving anything up. There is no sacrifice involved. You are removing something from your life that has made you miserable.

THERE IS NOTHING TO FEAR

You're trading lack of control over your gambling for total control: no choice for absolute choice. Like the cigarette for the smoker and the bottle for the drinker, part of you feels that gambling is your friend, your constant companion and crutch. Get it clearly into your mind, this is an illusion. In reality it's your worst enemy and, far from supporting you, it's driving you deeper and deeper into misery. You instinctively know this, so open your mind and follow your instincts.

REMOVE ALL DOUBTS

Think about all the good things you stand to gain by overcoming your gambling problem. Think of the enormous self-respect you'll regain and the time and energy you'll save, not only by stopping gambling but also by becoming free from all the deception, dodging your creditors, deceiving your friends and family and lying to yourself that you're in control.

That little boost you feel every time you gamble is how a non-gambler feels all the time, and how you'll feel all the time when you're free. Wouldn't you rather feel like that, without any effort or cost and without the horrible lows that gambling brings?

If you saw a heroin addict suffering the misery of drug addiction, would you advise them to keep injecting heroin into their veins? Of course you wouldn't. You would see that the 'high' they think they're getting is nothing more than relief from the craving that's caused by the drug as it leaves the body. It would be obvious to you that the only way to escape that craving permanently is to stop taking the drug.

> *Depend on the rabbit's foot if you will, but always remember, it didn't work for the rabbit.*
> **R. E. Shay (writer)**

Perhaps you think I'm over-dramatising the situation by comparing gambling to heroin addiction. I assure you, all addicts are caught in the same trap. See yourself as you would see a heroin addict and give yourself the only logical piece of advice:

IT'S TIME TO STOP!

Gamblers fail to see the solution as simple because they suffer from the tug-of-war of fear. Once you can see that there's nothing to fear, that you're not giving up anything or depriving yourself in any way, stopping becomes easy.

We have established that gambling does absolutely nothing positive for you whatsoever, that the beliefs that have imprisoned you in the gambling trap are merely illusions and that you have everything to gain and nothing to lose by stopping. There's nothing to fear. Life will become infinitely more enjoyable the moment you escape from the trap.

Perhaps you're afraid that the process of stopping will be traumatic. You may have struggled to quit before by using willpower and found it a tortuous experience. That's because the willpower method doesn't work. It leaves you feeling deprived, and so, as I will explain in the next chapter, you never really become completely free.

As you read this book and absorb it, I want you to think about everything we've established so far and make sure that you understand and accept it. If you have any doubts, re-read the relevant section until it becomes clear.

People sometimes say they understand everything, yet they retain a desire to gamble. They may think they have understood, but if they retain that desire then it's clear that the information hasn't gelled in their mind. They have missed something somewhere along the line and it's essential for them to go back and identify where the problem lies. It's often that they haven't truly opened their mind. If you follow the method, you'll no longer feel the desire to gamble. Remove the desire and the prison door will spring open.

> *True luck consists not in holding the best of the cards at the table; luckiest he who knows just when to rise and go home*
>
> **John Ray (academic)**

SUMMARY

- Addiction causes a tug-of-war of fear.
- The fear of failure is irrational.
- The fear of success is based on an illusion.
- Stop gambling and the fears go too.
- There's nothing to fear.

Chapter 8

WILLPOWER

IN THIS CHAPTER
•TAKING THE DIFFICULT OPTION •HOW WEAK-WILLED ARE YOU?
•THE WILLPOWER METHOD – A NEVER-ENDING STRUGGLE
•BECOMING FREE THE EASY WAY

If you think you have failed to solve your gambling problems before now because you lack the willpower, think again. Using willpower is more likely to make your problems worse.

PUSH OPEN THE DOOR

If it's so easy to stop gambling, then why do so many people find it incredibly hard? The reason is quite simple: they're using the wrong method.

The simplest of tasks becomes difficult if you go about it the wrong way. Think about opening a door. You push on the handle and it swings open with the minimum of effort. But have you ever tried pushing on the wrong side where the hinges are? You meet with instant resistance. The door might budge a tiny bit, but it won't swing open. It requires a huge amount of effort and determination. Push on the correct side and the door opens without you even having to think about it.

Most gamblers find it difficult to stop because they use the willpower method. They endure a constant conflict of will, a mental tug-of-war. On one side, your reason knows you should stop gambling because it's costing you a fortune, controlling your life and causing you misery. On the other side, your addiction makes you panic at the thought of being deprived of your pleasure or crutch. With the willpower method, you focus on all the reasons for stopping and hope you can last for long enough without gambling, for the desire to do so eventually to go.

The problem with this is that you still perceive gambling as a pleasure or crutch and therefore you feel you've made a sacrifice. So you force yourself into a self-imposed tantrum, just like a child being deprived of its toys. This feeling of deprivation makes you miserable, which in turn makes you want to try to cheer yourself up by doing the one thing you've vowed not to do – gamble again.

> *In a bet there is a fool and a thief.*
> **Proverb**

You only need willpower to stop if you have a conflict of will. We are going to resolve that conflict by removing one side of the tug-of-war, so that all your will is against gambling. Using willpower for the rest of your life to try not to gamble is unlikely to prove successful and will not make you happy; removing the desire to gamble will.

ALLEN CARR'S EASYWAY REMOVES THE NEED FOR WILLPOWER BY REMOVING THE ILLUSION THAT YOU'RE MAKING A SACRIFICE

Some people do manage to quit gambling through sheer force of will, but they never actually break free from their addiction, as I will explain in a moment. In most cases, the willpower method fails and you end up back in the trap feeling more miserable than before.

ENCOURAGING SOMEONE TO QUIT THROUGH THE USE OF WILLPOWER IS LIKE TELLING THEM TO OPEN A DOOR BY PUSHING ON THE HINGES

HOW WEAK-WILLED ARE YOU?

The willpower method is commonly assumed to be the only way to overcome an addiction and those who fail to quit are generally branded as weak-willed. Indeed, they often brand themselves as weak-willed. Perhaps you think that's why you've been unable to quit up until now: because you lack the strength of will. If that's the case, then you haven't yet understood the nature of the trap you're in.

Ask yourself whether you're weak-willed in other ways. Perhaps you're a smoker or you eat or drink too much, and you regard these conditions as further evidence of a weak will. There's a connection between all addictions, but the connection isn't that they're signs of a lack of willpower.

On the contrary, they're more likely evidence of a strong will. What they all share is that they're traps created by misleading information and untruths. And one of the most misleading and damaging untruths is that quitting requires willpower.

IN HIS OWN WORDS: MALIK

I went into business on my own when I was still in my teens. I learned fast and did very well. By the age of 25 I had made my first million. It wasn't easy. When you're young it's difficult to get people to take you seriously, so I had to work very hard and fight for everything I wanted. I had a flair for business but my real strength was my determination. I never let any problem defeat me.

Some people would call me a workaholic but I just enjoyed building up the business, so it didn't feel like work to me. I started gambling, initially as something to do for fun at the weekend. Money wasn't a problem so I didn't really feel it financially when I lost, but it did make me want to go back and get some sort of payback.

Then I had a blow with the business. I got a big tax bill that I hadn't planned for and things suddenly became pretty tight. I looked at my outgoings and realised I was getting through close to a grand a month on gambling alone. I'd had no idea. I told myself I had to stop, but when the weekend came round I felt this tremendous urge to gamble again. Despite telling myself that I could no longer afford it, I just couldn't make myself stop.

For the first time in my life, I was faced with something I couldn't control however much I tried. I couldn't understand it and it made me angry and resentful. I could see all the arguments for stopping,

I would tell myself each weekend that this would be the time I quit, and yet when it came to it a little voice said, 'Go on, you've worked hard all week, you deserve it,' and like a mug, I went along with it.

Afterwards I would feel really miserable. I felt like a complete failure and every Monday I would go back to work with a feeling of despair. Then I'd started hearing the voice during the week too: 'Go on, cheer yourself up. You can handle it.' Soon I was gambling seven days a week and I found myself filing for bankruptcy.

I was almost suicidal. I had worked so hard to build up a business all by myself and now I had thrown it all away. And for what? Absolutely nothing as far as I could see. In hindsight I now know where I was going wrong. I thought I was being weak-willed when, in fact, it was my strength of will to keep gambling that was overriding all the logical reasons to stop. Deep down I believed that gambling was a reward that I deserved for all my hard work, and the thought of giving it up seemed like too much of a sacrifice.

I've now quit gambling, built my business up again and am happier than ever. There was no sacrifice after all.

It takes a strong-willed person to persist in doing something that goes against all their instincts. You know that gambling is causing financial problems, making you increasingly stressed and unhappy, threatening to destroy your relationships, your career, your life, and yet you continue to do it. That isn't the behaviour of a weak-willed person.

Organising your life so you can sneak off to the bookie's or the casino without arousing suspicion; getting up early in the morning or staying up late at night so you can gamble online without your family knowing; ducking and diving to avoid your creditors; making up elaborate stories to borrow more money from other people; sacrificing the pastimes you used to enjoy because all your money is going on gambling: all these actions take a strong will.

If I saw you trying to open a door by pushing on the hinges and I told you you'd find it easier if you pushed on the handle, but you ignored me and insisted on pushing on the hinges, I'd call you wilful, not weak-willed.

Think of all the people you know who've had gambling problems. It's probably a small list because nobody likes to admit it. But there are enough high-profile examples to illustrate the fact that problem gambling isn't exclusive to the weak-willed.

> *The only man who makes money following the races is one who does it with a broom and shovel.*
> **Elbert Hubbard (writer and philosopher)**

Probably the most famous and insightful novel on the subject of gambling is *The Gambler* by Fyodor Dostoyevsky. The Russian wrote from experience, having himself endured the misery of gambling addiction. This was the same Dostoyevsky who also wrote the masterpiece *Crime and Punishment*, a novel of more than 650 pages, and survived four years chained up in a Siberian prison. Weak-willed? Hardly.

Ernest Hemingway was another writer with a gambling addiction and he was renowned for his competitive, strong and single-minded character. The same is true of anyone who reaches the top of their field in sport, yet many sportsmen and women succumb to problem gambling. Basketball star Charles Barclay reckons he gambled away $10 million. That's nothing compared to golfer John Daly, who puts his gambling losses somewhere between $50m and $60m.

> *In most betting shops you'll see three windows marked 'Bet Here', but only one window with the legend 'Pay Out'.*
>
> **Jeffrey Bernard**
> **(journalist)**

Singer Gladys Knight battled against an addiction to baccarat that saw her lose $60,000 in one night. Many other stars of stage and screen have suffered from problem gambling but have yet to admit to their condition because of the stigma.

The common ground between all these people is that they reached a position in their careers that required a very strong will. So why would their willpower fail them in this one area?

I'm sure you can also find evidence that you too are strong-willed. How do you react when people tell you that you have to change your ways and sort out your gambling problem? Don't you find you tend to do the opposite? Wouldn't you describe that as wilful? Do you think of yourself as weak-willed in any other areas that are not related to gambling or any other addiction?

Ironically, very strong-willed people can find it particularly hard to quit using the willpower method, because just like strong-willed children who have been deprived of their toys they'll keep their tantrum going for longer and at a greater intensity, whereas a weaker-willed person will get tired of moping sooner.

IN HER OWN WORDS: PAULA

I managed to stop gambling for six months once. I changed my whole routine to avoid going anywhere near the casino and I banned myself from going on the internet at all. It took huge willpower to stick to my regime and I reckoned that eventually it would get easier. In fact, it got harder the longer it went on and after six months I caved in.

It wasn't like a wound that healed, it was like a pain that kept getting worse. I felt a great sense of relief when I allowed myself to bet again but it didn't make me happy. What made it worse was that I punished myself with the thought that, had I persevered for longer, I might have succeeded. I felt like I'd run a marathon but collapsed a hundred yards short of the finishing line.

I now realise I was nowhere near the finishing line. In fact, there was no finishing line. I'd have just continued moping indefinitely. Thank goodness, I've now quit with Allen Carr's Easyway and the amazing thing is it took no willpower at all. I felt free right from the start.

When you try to quit by the willpower method, the struggle never ends. As long as you continue to believe that you're giving something up, you'll continue to feel deprived. The stronger your will, the longer you'll withstand the agony. Paula was strong-willed enough to hold out for six months, but the agony only got worse, because the longer she went on suffering a sense of deprivation, the more powerful her craving for gambling became.

CROSSING THE LINE THE EASY WAY

With Easyway, the elation of crossing the finishing line occurs as soon as you remove the fears and illusions that have kept you gambling. That's when you're free of the addiction. You need to understand that you will not get to that line by forcing yourself to suffer.

As I explained in Chapter 4, rather than helping you to quit, using the willpower method virtually ensures that you remain trapped because:

1. It reinforces the myth that quitting is hard and, therefore, adds to your fear.

2. It involves a feeling of deprivation, which you'll seek to alleviate in your usual way – by gambling.

Once you have failed using the willpower method, it's even more daunting to try again, because, like Paula, you'll have reinforced the illusion that it's impossible to get free.

People who have tried the willpower method and failed will often tell you they felt an enormous sense of relief when they first gave in. It's important to understand that this relief is nothing more than a temporary end to self-inflicted suffering. They don't think, 'Great! I've fallen back into the gambling trap.' It's not a pleasure. In fact, it's accompanied by feelings of failure and foreboding, guilt and disappointment.

OTHER QUITTERS

You may know people who are trying to overcome gambling or some other addiction by using willpower. You probably admire their determination and wish you could do the same. DON'T. Remember what I have told you about the willpower method and see things as they really are.

People who try to quit by the willpower method can put others off trying to stop since they reinforce the misconception that quitting means suffering and deprivation.

It's important that you ignore the advice of anyone who claims to have quit by the willpower method. The beautiful truth is there's no sacrifice. You're soon to become a happy non-gambler. To do that, you need to understand that you're not giving anything up. You only need willpower if you're caught in the tug-of-war of fear. Remove the fear and there's no conflict. It's easy.

Paula was waiting for the moment when her misery ended and she became a happy non-gambler. But, as she subsequently discovered with Easyway, there's nothing to wait for. You become a happy non-gambler the moment you unravel all the illusions that have led you into the gambling trap, free yourself from fear and stop gambling with a feeling of excitement and elation.

If you've followed the method so far and understood that the perceptions that have made you a slave to gambling are illusions; that you don't need willpower to stop; and that there's nothing to fear; you should already be feeling a sense of excitement and anticipation. It's natural to be a little nervous, don't worry about that. You have already taken a major step in solving your gambling problem. You can very soon start living your life again free from the misery of being a gambler. You are taking back control and soon you will be free.

> *You know, horses are smarter than we are. You never heard of a horse going broke betting on people.*
>
> **Will Rogers (cowboy)**

Isn't that worth celebrating?

There's only one more obstacle that could be preventing you from feeling this sense of elation. Not everyone who tries and fails to stop by using the willpower method concludes that they're weak-willed, but rather than look for the true reasons why they remain hooked, they decide it must be down to another aspect of their personality over which they have no control. When all other explanations fail them, there's one theory that conveniently provides the excuse they need to avoid having to face up to their problem. In the next chapter we will address the 'addictive personality'.

SUMMARY

- Stopping is only hard if you use the wrong method.

- Gambling addiction isn't a sign of being weak-willed. It's often the opposite.

- With the willpower method, you never become completely free.

- With Easyway, you become free the moment you reverse the brainwashing and stop.

Chapter 9

THE ADDICTIVE
PERSONALITY

The theory of the addictive personality stems from looking at the situation from the wrong perspective. The typical character traits shared by addicts aren't the cause of their addiction, they're the result.

Most gamblers are baffled as to why they continue to behave in ways that cause so much harm. Until they're able to understand the nature of the trap they're in and how it controls them, they're left feeling helpless and foolish. In order to combat this feeling, they make up excuses in a vain attempt to explain why they keep gambling despite the damage it's causing:

'I don't earn much. It's my only chance of getting rich.'

'I've been unlucky recently, but that's bound to change.'

'It's my only pleasure.'

'I've had a hard time at home lately. I need an escape.'

When it's pointed out that their problem is an addiction to gambling, they're ready with the excuse:

'I have an addictive personality.'

Despite the knowledge that millions of people in the world are suffering from the same addiction to gambling, they think that their own problem is singular to them. This is why talking is so important. When you come out of your cocoon and speak to people about your problems and discover that they're experiencing, or have experienced, exactly what you're going through, then you begin to see that addiction isn't a weakness in the individual.

Many addicts believe that there must be something in their genetic make-up that makes them more susceptible than others to becoming hooked, and makes it harder or even impossible for them to escape. It's a convenient excuse, but all it does is ensure that they remain forever trapped, their suffering increasing and the misery leading them further and further into despair.

Sadly, their misconception is backed up by so-called experts, who support the theory of the addictive personality. The term is bandied about so often that it's easy to be fooled into believing it's an established condition. It's not. It's a theory, largely based on the incidence of multiple addictions in the same people, e.g. gamblers who are also smokers or alcoholics, or heroin addicts who smoke and are heavily in debt.

All these addictions are caused by the same thing, but it's not your personality: it's the misguided belief that the thing you're addicted to gives you a genuine pleasure or crutch. Remember:

THE MISERY OF THE ADDICT ISN'T RELIEVED BY THE THING THEY'RE ADDICTED TO, IT'S CAUSED BY IT

The fear of failure drives people with a gambling problem to seek reasons to avoid even trying to quit. The addictive personality theory gives them the perfect excuse. If you think you have an addictive personality, you may regard quitting as an impossible task. 'How can I override my own genetic make-up?' This illusion can also be reinforced by your failed attempts to quit by using willpower.

It's further confirmed by people who have quit by using the willpower method and are feeling deprived because they still believe they're making a sacrifice. After all, if they have abstained for years and are still craving their little crutch, surely there must be some flaw in their genetic make-up?

PEOPLE WHO WHINGE ABOUT HAVING QUIT ARE CONSTANTLY TORMENTED BECAUSE THEY STILL BELIEVE THAT THEY ARE DEPRIVING THEMSELVES BY 'GIVING UP' A GENUINE PLEASURE OR CRUTCH

You now know that you're not 'giving up' anything. Pleading an addictive personality is just another cop-out. You don't want to stay trapped in your life as a gambler with all the fear, misery and hardship that goes with it – that's why you're reading this book. You have made the decision to escape and you're well on the way to doing just that.

It's easy, provided you keep an open mind. If you cling to the excuse that you have an addictive personality, it means that your mind isn't open and you risk sentencing yourself to remain in the prison for the rest of your life.

I used to think that my addiction to smoking must be something I'd inherited from my father who was also a heavy smoker and died of lung cancer. To an observer I must have looked like I was happily going to an early grave, puffing on cigarettes all the way. In truth, I was desperate to quit. I was terrified of the threat of lung cancer and a slow, painful death. But I felt stupid and helpless because all my attempts had failed, and so putting it down to a flaw in my personality seemed to offer the only rational explanation.

I now know that I was not stupid, that the spread of misinformation is so pervasive that anybody can be conned, and most people are to some extent. But once you understand how addiction really works, the illusions disappear and you realise that you're complete without your illusory 'crutch'. With it, you're a slave.

DEGREES OF ADDICTION

So why do some people fall deeper into the trap than others? Why can one person have the occasional 'flutter' and walk away, while another ends up gambling away everything they own and more? Doesn't that suggest that one has an addictive personality and the other doesn't?

It does point to a difference between them, yes, but there are numerous differences between people which can explain why one's behaviour differs from another's in this context, and none of them has anything to with an addictive personality.

Some people find their first experience of betting unrewarding, and so they don't feel inclined to do it again. Some people are simply too busy to find the time to gamble. Others know they can't afford to gamble more than a small amount each week and try to discipline themselves to limit it to that. In addition to that, our behaviour is closely linked to the influences we are subjected to as we grow up: different parents, teachers, friends, the things we read, watch and listen to, the places we go, the people we meet, etc.

> In the casino, the cardinal rule is to keep them playing and to keep them coming back. The longer they play, the more they lose, and in the end, we get it all.
> **Ace Rothstein,**
> **Casino (film, 1995)**

All these factors will have a bearing on how quickly we descend into the trap. The celebrities that I mentioned before fell rapidly because they had millions to lose as well as the time and opportunity to do so.

AN AFFINITY BETWEEN WEAKNESSES

Have you ever noticed how you and other gamblers seem to be a different breed from everyone else? Do you appear to share similar character traits: an unstable temperament, which swings between exuberance and misery; a tendency towards excess; a high susceptibility to stress; evasiveness, anxiety, insecurity? Do you feel more comfortable in their company?

The temptation is to believe that these character traits are evidence of the addictive personality that led you into the gambling trap. But did you exhibit them before you got hooked? Or is it the case that they are the *result* of being in the trap?

The reason addicts feel more comfortable in the company of similar addicts is not because they're more interesting or fun; on the contrary, the attraction lies in the very fact that they won't challenge you or make you think twice about your addiction because they're in the same boat. All addicts know that they're doing something stupid and self-destructive. If they're surrounded by other people doing the same thing, they don't feel quite so idiotic.

The good news is that, once you're free from the addiction, the harmful effects it has had on your character will also disappear.

THE EVIDENCE OF HISTORY

If there were a gene that predisposed people to become addicts, you would expect the percentage of addicts in the world to have remained fairly constant throughout history. Yet this isn't the case. Take smoking: in the 1940s over 80 per cent of the UK adult male population was hooked on nicotine; today it's under 25 per cent. A similar trend is evident throughout most of western Europe and the United States. So are we to conclude that the proportion of people with addictive personalities has fallen by a whopping 55 per cent in just over half a century?

At the same time, the number of smokers in Asia has soared.

What complex genetic anomaly is this that rises and falls so rapidly, and even appears to transfer itself wholesale from one continent to another?

EFFECT NOT CAUSE

You didn't become addicted to gambling because you have an addictive personality. If you think you have an addictive personality, it's simply because you got addicted to gambling.

This is the trick that addiction plays on you. It makes you feel that you're dependent on your addiction and that there's some weakness in your character or genetic make-up. It maintains its grip on you by distorting your perceptions.

The addictive personality theory encourages the belief that escape is out of your hands and that you're condemned to a life of slavery and misery. Remember, you didn't feel the need or desire to gamble until you started gambling. It was gambling that created the addiction, not the other way round.

The reason many people have multiple addictions is that all addictions leave you feeling dissatisfied, and so the tendency is to search for yet something else to fill the void. Also many people switch from one addiction to another because they're using willpower to quit, and so feel the need for a substitute. None of this has anything to do with an addictive personality. Even if you were to to have an addictive personality, that wouldn't mean you would find it harder to quit; it would simply mean that you would be more likely to get hooked in the first place. Since you're already hooked, it's irrelevant. Millions of addicts who were convinced they had an adddictive personality have got free with Easyway and so will you.

Gambling addiction will soon be behind you. Once you can strip away the illusions and see the situation in its true light, you'll wonder how you were ever conned into seeing it differently. Like millions of people around the world, you've been the victim of an ingenious trap. Recognise the trap for what it is and you'll be ready to walk free.

SUMMARY

- The addictive personality theory gives the addict an excuse to avoid even trying to escape.

- The personality traits shared by addicts are caused by their addiction; they're not the cause of the addiction.

- Even if you were to have an addictive personality, Easyway will work for you.

Chapter 10

GETTING HOOKED

IN THIS CHAPTER
• *WHY WE START GAMBLING* • *COMPELLING INFLUENCES*
• *TRYING TO GET HOOKED* • *THE FUTILE PURSUIT OF FULFILMENT*
• *THE FOURTH INSTRUCTION*

In order fully to understand the trap you're in and how to escape it, you need to understand how you fell into it in the first place.

We have established that the difficulty gamblers have in stopping has nothing to do with an addictive personality or a lack of willpower, but is caused by illusions, which trap us in a prison of fear. You may be wondering, then, why it is that some people become hooked and others don't?

We all go through different experiences in life. I've explained about the void and how it's created. The comfort we seek during childhood makes us vulnerable to disillusionment and insecurity. These feelings create an emptiness that we feel the need to fill.

Because we all have different experiences as we grow up, we all experience the void to differing degrees and some people feel more affected by it than others. It tends to start during our teenage years: this is the time when we are making the biggest transition, from childhood to adulthood, and are, therefore, most vulnerable to disillusionment and insecurity; it's also the time when the common stimulants – drinking, smoking, gambling – become legal, and so are more readily available. Not surprisingly, this is the time of life when most addicts get hooked.

Of course, there are plenty of people who don't become addicts in their teenage years, but that doesn't mean they won't later in life. Most non-addicts assume that addicts must get *some* benefit from their behaviour because otherwise they wouldn't be doing it. Sometimes all it takes is a crisis, such as a car accident or a bereavement, for people to turn to smoking, drinking, gambling, etc., in the belief that it will provide some comfort.

Plenty of people who have become smokers or drinkers in their thirties or forties come to our clinics to quit, and it doesn't take long to establish that they've spent their entire lives believing that smoking or drinking could give them some pleasure or benefit. They didn't get hooked sooner because their desire had never been enough to outweigh their knowledge of the dangers. One trauma was enough to tip the balance.

It makes perfect sense that when we feel sad or traumatised we should try to make ourselves feel better by giving ourselves some form of pleasure or crutch. The baffling question is: why do we believe that we will get that pleasure or crutch from things we know to be harmful, like smoking, drinking and gambling? The simple answer is: that's what we are told from an early age.

It's not just the advertisers and marketing people who feed us this lie. The biggest influences are the people we regard as allies, foremost among them being our own parents.

Is it any wonder that we try to make ourselves feel better by gambling when we grow up seeing our parents and other adults do exactly the same? They might preach to us about the dangers of becoming hooked and losing everything, but the next minute they go and buy a lottery ticket or place a bet on a horse race. I explained earlier how we also tend to copy the celebrities who become our role models.

With the exception of the high-profile problem gamblers I mentioned in Chapter 7, I am unaware of any celebrities campaigning to raise awareness of the dangers of gambling. On the contrary, they reinforce the myth that gambling is good by making it part of their high society lifestyle.

> *A race track is a place where windows clean people.*
> **Danny Thomas (actor and comedian)**

We are drawn to celebrities because we covet their lifestyle, so it follows that we are drawn to the things they do. In recent years, gambling has become an increasingly popular way for high earners to show off their wealth and more and more of them have been caught in the gambling trap.

Another major influence is friends who gamble. I can think of several friends of mine who gamble on the football results and they all present the same positive image of what they're doing. It consists mainly of the following traits:

• **Studiousness** – they study the form and think carefully about their predictions.

• **Excitement** – they become very focused when the results come in and they're checking them off against their betting slip.

• **Humour** – they laugh when they win and when they lose, giving the impression that it doesn't really matter to them either way.

These are all traits that I would like to have, so it would be easy for me to conclude that gambling would be good for me. Fortunately, I know an addict when I see one and it's obvious to me that all these traits are a front.

• They may study the form and think carefully about their predictions, but they know that it's really all in the lap of the gods.

• The excitement they show is a combination of anxiety and impatience. It's like someone expecting bad news; they fidget, they watch the clock, they get annoyed by false dawns and they become incapable of conversation or anything that diverts them from their bet.

• The laughter is a classic sign of denial. When they win,

it's nothing more than relief; when they lose, it covers up their disappointment.

I also know that these friends do not gamble life-changing sums of money. Not yet anyway. Therefore, they stand to make no really significant gain even if they were to be lucky. It's obvious to me that the only reason they gamble is because they're addicted to it.

But now that you understand the nature of the addict and the trap, you never need to be taken in by other gamblers again. You can see them for what they are: slaves to their addiction.

THE HIDDEN MESSAGE

In a strange way, the negative messages we are given about gambling and other harmful activities can actually influence us in their favour. Why is it not enough for me to tell you that gambling is dangerous and provide examples that prove the point? For the same reason that telling teenagers motorcycles are dangerous does not deter them.

The answer lies in the attraction of transgression. During our teenage years, we discover that some of the things we've been warned against seem pleasurable. This sows a seed in our mind: we suspect that this might be the case with other things we've been warned against. Then we see people apparently enjoying those very things and our suspicions are confirmed.

'OK, so cigarettes can kill, in that case there must be something really fantastic about them to make all these people smoke despite that danger.'

'OK, so gambling can leave you destitute, but it must be great fun for people to take that risk – anyway, I can control it.'

Rather than take the warnings at face value, we look for a hidden message: 'If people are doing it in spite of all the dangers we've been warned about, there must be something great about it.' So we form a desire to experiment.

The simple truth, which we are never told, is that all those people – the celebrities, the friends, our parents – are doing it because they too have been brainwashed. They're playing with fire and in some cases end up finding they get their fingers badly burnt.

WHY WE CONTINUE TO GAMBLE

We take up gambling because we assume it must be pleasurable. We're not sure what that pleasure is but we don't want to miss out, so we try it. But if, as I say, there's no genuine pleasure in gambling, why do we continue to do it?

Think about smokers. Perhaps you are one. The first time you smoke a cigarette it tastes foul. For some people, that's enough to persuade them never to try another. But most don't give up so easily. Remember what I said about addicts being strong-willed. They're convinced that there's some amazing pleasure to be had from smoking and if they didn't experience it the first time, well, they'll just have to try harder.

The same applies to gambling. If you don't get a kick from it the first time, you assume that you haven't pushed yourself far enough. So you gamble again and you gamble more. You've entered the trap.

THE REASON YOU CONTINUE TO GAMBLE IS THAT YOU ARE CHASING AN IMPOSSIBLE GOAL

I'll call that goal fulfilment – the sense that everything has been restored and you can walk away happy. Gamblers never feel fulfilled, even if they win. That's why, win or lose, they always feel the need to have another bet. Fulfilment would be having no further desire to gamble.

In other words, the fulfilment a gambler is seeking is the way a non-gambler feels all the time. The only way you can find that is not to gamble. Addiction to gambling creates a void, which we try to fill through the act of gambling. However, each bet, far from ending the empty feeling, merely ensures that we suffer it again and again.

While the horses or dogs are running, the roulette wheel is spinning or the hand of cards is being played, for that moment gamblers are close to the sense of fulfilment that non-gamblers feel all the time and take for granted. That's because they're partially and temporarily relieving the void caused by their addiction.

So, for a few moments, paradoxically, they feel like a non-gambler. Remember:

THE ONLY WAY YOU CAN TRULY FEEL LIKE A NON-GAMBLER IS NOT TO GAMBLE

Ask a gambler about the feelings that drive them to gamble and the answers will be very similar to those given by a smoker:

• **Boredom** – 'It's something to do.'

• **Company** – 'It helps me forget that I'm alone.'

• **Stress** – 'It helps me to relax.'

• **Routine** – 'It's just a habit.'

• **Reward** – 'It's my little indulgence.'

In none of these cases does pleasure come into it. I enjoy playing golf. If I could, I would play much more often. I wouldn't wait until I felt bored or lonely or stressed. I would break my routine for a game of golf. And I don't feel I have to earn the right to play. I actively pursue it because it gives me pleasure and it's good for me.

> *Even as I approach the gambling hall, as soon as I hear, two rooms away, the jingle of money poured out on the table, I almost go into convulsions.*
> **Fyodor Dostoyevsky (writer)**

Addicts often talk about their 'drug' in terms of a 'reward'. But why would you reward yourself with something that damages your health and wealth? And what sort of reward is it that, when you're doing it, you wish you weren't? It's only when you're not doing it that it seems so precious.

When you gamble it temporarily quietens the Little Monster,

creating the illusion that gambling has made you relaxed and happy. In fact, all it has done is taken you from feeling uneasy to feeling okay. Before you created the Little Monster you felt okay anyway, you didn't feel uncomfortable when you were not gambling. Now you feel the need to do it again and again, with a bigger and bigger 'fix', just to get back to a level where you feel okay.

FIX FIXATION

It's revealing that junkies use the word 'fix'. A fix is a solution to a problem; you fix something that is broken. A fix isn't an improvement. It's not a pleasure or reward. It's nothing more than relief, like wearing tight shoes for the feeling when you take them off.

DENIAL AND ACCEPTANCE

All problem gamblers wish they could be non-gamblers. At the same time they're afraid to 'give up' their little pleasure or crutch. This conflict leaves them feeling helpless, frustrated and stupid. They don't understand the trap they're in and feel powerless to resolve their dilemma.

As a result, they tend to bury their head in the sand and deny they have a problem. They lie to themselves about the state they're in and pretend that all they're doing is having a bit of harmless fun. 'It's just a game.' If that were the case, why not play for nothing? Because it's the emotional response to the possibility of winning or losing money that triggers the physical response in the brain that feeds the Little Monster. Without that response, there's not even the illusion of pleasure.

The beautiful truth is any gambler can stop easily, painlessly and permanently, provided they understand the trap they're in and follow the method set out in this book. And that includes you.

You've already taken a big step. You've overcome denial and accepted that you have a gambling problem. That's why you're reading this book. Now all we have to do is remove the illusions that make one part of your mind want to gamble.

> *If you're playing poker and look round the table and can't tell who the sucker is, it's you.*
> **Paul Newman (actor)**

I've explained how gambling provides no genuine pleasure or crutch, it merely creates the illusion of pleasure. Your belief in the illusion of pleasure is what got you into the trap. Now that you understand the nature of the trap, you can see that there's no pleasure, just a steady slide into abject misery. You understand that gambling does not fill the void, it creates it.

YOU HAVE ALREADY BEGUN TO REMOVE THE BRAINWASHING

It's essential that you're not diverted from your path. There are several things that could hinder your escape, so let's address these so that success is guaranteed. Perhaps there's a part of you that still believes you get some pleasure or a crutch from gambling.

Throwing it away

Described as the 'crack cocaine' of the betting industry, Fixed Odds Betting Terminals (FOBTs) arrived in the UK in 2001 and have spearheaded a rapid increase in the number of betting shops across the country. These high-stakes, high-speed machines allow punters to bet up to £100 a spin at fixed odds – each spin takes 20 seconds. There are proposals to limit the maximum amount you can stake. The 35,000 machines currently in operation return a minimum of £1.8bn in profit to British bookmakers annually as well as large sums in tax.

Perhaps you're afraid that life without gambling will leave you feeling deprived in some way. There are many sources of information that can mislead you with misconceptions like these, and some of them are well meaning. Please take note of my next instruction:

THE FOURTH INSTRUCTION
IGNORE ALL ADVICE AND INFLUENCES THAT
CONFLICT WITH EASYWAY

The truth is you're not 'giving up' anything. Instead, you're freeing yourself from a trap that has been causing you misery and threatening everything you value. Soon you'll be free from that nightmare. The desire to gamble will be removed and you'll be a happy non-gambler. Now that's something to get excited about!

SUMMARY

- Role models make the illusion of pleasure more convincing.
- Gambling works like an addictive drug.
- The only way to feel like a non-gambler is not to gamble.
- Ignore any advice or influences that conflict with Easyway.

Chapter 11

INSTANT FIXES

IN THIS CHAPTER
•HABIT OR ADDICTION?
•HOW TO FEEL LIKE A NON-GAMBLER
•SMOKING AND DRINKING •WELL-MEANING FRIENDS

The belief that you're dependent on gambling for pleasure or a crutch isn't only the cause of your continued addiction to gambling, it can also lead to other addictions.

A huge industry has grown up around smokers who want to quit but are afraid that they'll find it too hard to go without their little crutch. This industry sells substitute nicotine products, the theory being that you first break the 'habit' of smoking by ceasing to smoke, but at the same time you keep your nicotine withdrawal at bay by taking nicotine via another source. Then, having broken the 'habit', you wean yourself off the nicotine.

Of course, it doesn't work. In fact, people who use nicotine products usually end up more addicted in the long run. Good for the manufacturers of nicotine products, not so good for nicotine addicts who want to be free of their addiction. So much for substitutes!

Smoking isn't a habit, it's an addiction, and just as the only reason a junkie sticks a needle into his arm is to get the heroin, the only reason a smoker smokes is to get the nicotine. Take the nicotine out of cigarettes and the illusion of pleasure disappears immediately.

Even addicts who sense they get no genuine pleasure from gambling, smoking, etc., still believe they need it to help them relax. They crave the feeling of relaxation that non-addicts have all the time. The only reason you gamble is to relieve the empty, insecure feeling of withdrawal, which non-gamblers don't suffer from in the first place.

THERE IS ONLY ONE WAY TO FEEL LIKE A NON-GAMBLER AND THAT IS TO BECOME ONE!

Some so-called experts will tell you it's difficult for addicts to quit because you have to conquer two powerful forces: the 'habit' and the awful withdrawal pangs. Based on this belief, the theory behind using substitutes appears to make sense. Rather than making life doubly hard for yourself, tackle the two powerful forces separately. While you're breaking the habit, keep the addiction fed. Then, once you've broken the habit, gradually wean yourself off the substitute.

Millions of people have followed this advice and they're still addicted. Why? Because the theory is based on two fatal flaws:

ADDICTION IS NOT THE SAME AS HABIT

THE PHYSICAL WITHDRAWAL IS EASY TO DEAL WITH ANYWAY

And so the two 'powerful forces' that you're told you have to conquer are actually non-existent.

For gamblers, there's no substitute on the market specifically designed to replicate the 'drug' effect of gambling without actually having to gamble. Gamblers are also unaware of the trap that they're in. The restless, insecure feeling they get when they're not gambling is the same feeling that smokers get when they're unable to smoke, alcoholics when they're unable to drink and heroin addicts when they can't get a fix. Non-addicts don't suffer from this feeling. It's caused by the last gamble, cigarette, drink or fix.

The greatest evil with all substitutes – and that includes anything you might give yourself to replace the 'reward' you believed you were getting from gambling – is that they perpetuate the illusion that quitting is hard and that you're 'giving up' something and therefore making a sacrifice. Get it clearly into your mind:

YOU'RE NOT 'GIVING UP' ANYTHING

All you're doing is getting rid of an evil that turned you into a slave and made your life a nightmare. You have no need to replace it with anything. When you get over a bout of flu, do you think, 'Okay, so what disease can I get now to take its place?' Of course not! You simply get on with your life happy that the problem is now behind you.

WELL-MEANING FRIENDS

People who care about you and know about your gambling problem may offer to help you financially. Resist the temptation to take them up on their kind offer.

People who don't understand the gambling trap see it primarily as a financial problem. They assume you've got into difficulties because you've had a run of bad luck, gone heavily into debt and you now think the only way to claw back your winnings is to gamble more. They can see the flaw in this logic, and they figure that by clearing your debts they'll remove your need to keep gambling.

But you know it's not the money that keeps you gambling, it's the addiction. All gamblers lie to themselves about the pleasure they get from gambling, but one thing that makes it harder for them to do so is the financial worry. Take that away and you take away a big incentive to quit.

> Nobody is always a winner and anybody who says he is is either a liar or doesn't play poker.
> **Amarillo Slim
> (poker player)**

Just as cigarette substitutes perpetuate the addiction by not tackling the cause, the same is true of financial bail-outs from well-meaning friends.

THE FIFTH INSTRUCTION
RESIST ANY PROMISE OF A TEMPORARY FIX

SUMMARY

- Gambling is not a habit, it is an addiction.
- Withdrawal is not a problem.
- You do not need a substitute for gambling.
- Remember, you're not 'giving up' anything.
- You can't control your addiction, it controls you.

CHAPTER 12

A FEW BIG QUESTIONS

IN THIS CHAPTER
• *HOW WILL I KNOW WHEN I'VE MADE MY LAST BET?*
• *WHEN DO I BECOME A NON-GAMBLER?*
• *WILL I EVER BE COMPLETELY FREE?* • *CAN I ENJOY LIFE WITHOUT GAMBLING?* • *WHAT DO I DO IN A CRISIS?*

You need complete certainty to become a happy non-gambler, so it's time to tackle some burning questions and replace doubt with understanding.

People with a gambling problem wish they didn't gamble but are also afraid that they'll have to go through some terrible trauma in order to quit and that they'll never be able to enjoy life without gambling. Even though they know that gambling is ruining their lives, these fears cause them to put off what they see as the evil day. 'I will stop, just not right now.'

It's no surprise that gamblers have these fears. All through our lives we are led to believe that gambling is fun and that addictions are incredibly hard to kick. These myths are ingrained in us before we even start to gamble. No wonder we find it difficult to believe that stopping can be easy once we're actually hooked.

Assuming you're eager to become a non-gambler and have

been following the method so far, you may be wondering how you'll know when you've achieved your goal? When will you be able to tell that you've definitely become a non-gambler?

• When you can go a whole day without gambling?

• When you can go a week?

• When you can enjoy watching a sports event without wanting to bet on it?

All these possibilities assume that you'll start off with a feeling of sacrifice or deprivation and be 'hanging in there', avoiding gambling. If you do that, there's no telling how long that will last. Remember, Easyway is different and doesn't involve feeling deprived or miserable, so the answer to the question, 'When will you be able to tell that you've definitely become a non-gambler?', is much more straightforward:

YOU BECOME A NON-GAMBLER THE MOMENT YOU MAKE THE DECISION NEVER TO GAMBLE AGAIN

When you pass an examination, such as a driving test, you experience a wonderful boost. You'll experience a similar and far greater boost when you quit gambling with Easyway. Doubt will be replaced by certainty and fear will be replaced by relief and elation.

It's not enough to *try* never to gamble again or *hope* that you'll never gamble again, you must be certain. If you're not, your doubts will grow and fester at the back of your mind.

People on the willpower method are always waiting for some sign of confirmation that they're free. They also spend their time suspecting that there could be bad news lurking just around the corner. It's like a dark shadow stalking their every move.

Imagine going for tests because you think you might have a terminal disease and being told that you'll have to wait months or years for the result. It would be torture. Hoping for good news, fearing bad news and spending every day worrying because you simply don't know for certain which it will be. Now imagine if you had to wait the rest of your life for those results. That's what it's like for people who aren't certain they've kicked gambling completely. They spend the rest of their lives waiting for something that they hope will never happen.

This is why the willpower method makes people so miserable. They have to endure the rest of their lives waiting for nothing to happen. Alternatively, they cave in and feel a bigger failure than when they started.

BELIEVING IS SUCCEEDING

Get it clearly into your mind: you won't miss gambling and you'll enjoy life more and be better equipped to cope with stress when you're free. Please don't misunderstand me. I'm NOT saying 'look at it this way' in the hope that you might be able to kid yourself that something genuinely very hard and difficult could actually be easy. I'm saying IT IS EASY TO STOP GAMBLING. It's just that you, and the people you might know who've tried to stop by using willpower, have gone about it the hard way up until now.

REPLACE CONFUSION WITH UNDERSTANDING

Different people reach this stage of the book in different frames of mind. Some think they understand everything and feel certain they're ready to quit. If that's you, I'm delighted, but it's still essential that you finish the book. If you're uncertain, don't worry, all will become clear. Whatever your current frame of mind, take the time and care to read right to the end.

It's perfectly understandable to believe that stopping gambling will be hard. There's nothing stupid or unusual in that belief. We're subjected to this brainwashing all our lives and then we reinforce it by trying to quit by using the willpower method. All your failed attempts to control your gambling have simply served to reinforce the belief that it has a powerful hold over you. However, that hold was the result of the illusion that gambling was doing something for you and providing you with a genuine pleasure or crutch. Once that illusion has been removed, the addiction loses its power and the situation is reversed. You then have the power to escape easily and permanently.

That desperate yearning and irritability you've suffered in the past when you've tried to stop by willpower may go against all logic but the feeling was still very real.

As addicts, we find ourselves in confusion. When we're forced to consider gambling logically, we can easily accept that it's a mug's game. Yet we still feel a desire to do it and that is what causes the mental tug-of-war. We feel that we get some pleasure or crutch from it but are not sure why.

The fact that we can't put our finger on what that boost is and don't really know why we have the desire does not mean it's difficult to understand. We don't understand it because we've been brainwashed with false information about it. And once we're hooked, the addiction seems to confirm the illusions of the brainwashing. Once these illusions have been removed, it's easy to see the reality.

> Last year people lost more than one billion dollars playing poker. And casinos made 27 billion just by being around those people.
>
> **Samantha Bee (author)**

You had no need to gamble before you started. You were brainwashed into believing that gambling was fun and, once you began, the addiction took hold and you found yourself becoming uncomfortable and ill at ease if you tried not to gamble. You assumed that this feeling of unease was caused by not gambling, but that can't be true because non-gamblers don't feel anxious or edgy when they can't gamble. It's gambling that creates that unease in the first place, then partially removes it to create the illusion of pleasure. You didn't suffer the unease before you started gambling and, with Easyway, you won't suffer it when you stop.

ONCE IS TOO MUCH

Such is the confusion surrounding gambling that many people believe that the occasional gamble does not make you a gambler. Get it clearly into your mind: if you gamble, you're a gambler. There's only one essential to being a non-gambler: not to gamble – ever!

REMEMBER, GAMBLING DOES NOT RELIEVE THE ANXIETY, IT CAUSES IT

The willpower method is all about combatting the desire to gamble, not removing it. In the first few days after quitting, when your willpower is at its strongest, you may have the upper hand in the battle. But having to use willpower is exhausting and frustrating, and sooner or later your resolve weakens and you start questioning your decision. You start thinking, 'Just one bet won't do any harm.' Of course, if you place that bet, you'll find yourself back in the trap again in no time at all.

You then have to make the other excuses, 'You've always got to have some vices', or 'I've just picked the wrong time', and it just goes on and on.

Is it surprising that we get so confused, irritable and downright miserable on the willpower method? It would be a miracle if we didn't!

If you're worried that you might fall back into the trap at some point after you've quit, remember that it's this tug-of-war that causes ex-gamblers to become gamblers again. Clear your mind of the illusions, remove the brainwashing and the tug-of-war will disappear.

GOOD TIMES

Gamblers fear that if they take gambling out of their life, they will take out the enjoyment too. It's easy to see why such a belief would stop anyone from trying to quit. Nobody wants to lead a life devoid of pleasure.

The truth is, gambling actually reduces your ability to derive enjoyment from genuine pleasures. A non-gambler can watch sport and enjoy the spectacle, the competition, the physical endeavour – all the aspects that make sport entertaining. For the gambler, sport becomes meaningless if they don't have money on it.

The brainwashing causes gamblers to have a romanticised idea of gambling. Where there have been genuinely enjoyable situations involving gambling, a quick analysis of all the details of these situations will reveal that there were other aspects that made it enjoyable: the presence of friends, an exciting location, a celebration of some kind, etc.

If you consider such occasions to have been enjoyable because you were gambling, analyse them carefully and understand why, although the gambling may have appeared to enhance the situation, in reality it did no such thing. Instead of fearing that such occasions won't be enjoyable again without gambling, remind yourself that you'll now be able to enjoy those situations more because you'll be free from the slavery of gambling.

Most of the time we're not even aware of how we feel while we're gambling. The only time we're really aware of how it makes us feel is when we want to gamble but can't, or we're gambling but wish we didn't have to.

What sort of pleasure or reward is it that, when you're doing it, you wish you weren't; it's only when you can't do it that it becomes so precious. Just watch people as they feed coin after coin into slot machines. Do

> *Dice have their own laws which the courts of justice cannot undo.*
> **St Ambrose (Bishop of Milan)**

they look as if they're having a good time? In fact they often seem more robotic than the machines themselves. These slot machine automatons are bored out of their minds, hardly conscious in fact. They seem like zombies who are utterly controlled by the machines into which they are pumping their money. There's clearly no pleasure in it at all.

BAD TIMES

Just as gamblers believe they get pleasure from gambling, they also believe it provides some sort of crutch. This is because they tend to turn to gambling at times of stress and regard it as a relief.

There are many stressful situations from which you might see gambling as an escape: a family row, pressure at work, even financial problems. You can take yourself away, focus on whatever you choose to gamble on and, briefly, put your problems out of your mind. However, it never really works as the problems remain niggling at the back of your mind and the consequences of continuing to spend your time gambling away more and more money create additional stress and increase your anxiety.

And sooner or later you have to return to the real world and the problems are still there. In fact, they've usually got worse. If you believe that gambling provides a crutch in these situations, what happens the next time such a situation arises after you've quit? Your brain will tell you, 'At times like this I would have had a bet.' And you'll feel deprived that you can no longer do so.

Think about it: have you ever found yourself in the midst of a domestic row and thought, 'It doesn't matter that we're hurling horrible insults at one another, that we seem to be so unhappy. Lucky me, I can just go and gamble and it'll be all right'? Or did the fact that you gamble make the row worse?

FIXED ODDS BETTING TERMINALS

FOTBs foster problem gambling even more than other slot machines because of their 'event frequency' – the speed at which you play and then bet again (problem gamblers tend to prefer fast, simple games which don't give them time to stop and think), the number of 'near wins' that occur and, of course, the higher stakes involved. The higher the payback, the more gamblers are encouraged to chase their losses.

Non-gamblers also have stressful situations in their lives but they're not left moping because they can't gamble. All you have to do is accept that, like everyone else, you'll have ups and downs in your life after you've quit, and understand that if you start wishing you could gamble in such situations, you'll be moping for an illusion and creating a void.

GAMBLING REDUCES YOUR ABILITY TO COPE WITH STRESSFUL SITUATIONS BY ADDING TO THE STRESS

Anticipate the difficult times in life after you've quit and prepare yourself mentally, so that you don't get caught out. Remind yourself that any stress you feel isn't because you can't gamble. Tell yourself, 'Okay, today may not be so great, but at least I haven't got the added problem of being a slave to gambling. I'm stronger now.' You'll find that the stressful situations in your life will actually feel less severe once you're free. In fact, life becomes a whole lot easier and a whole lot more fun. Being free enhances all situations in life. The good times are so much better and the bad times not nearly as bad.

THE SIXTH INSTRUCTION
GET IT CLEAR IN YOUR MIND: GAMBLING GIVES YOU NO GENUINE PLEASURE OR CRUTCH; YOU ARE NOT MAKING A SACRIFICE; THERE IS NOTHING TO GIVE UP AND NO REASON TO FEEL DEPRIVED

SUMMARY

• You become a non-gambler the moment you decide never to gamble again.

• Clear your mind of uncertainty.

• Remove the illusions, and the tug-of-war disappears.

• Gambling reduces your ability to enjoy life.

• Gambling doesn't relieve stress, it causes it.

• Once free, you'll enjoy the good times more and handle the bad times better.

CHAPTER 13

ALL GAMBLERS ARE THE SAME

IN THIS CHAPTER
•WOMEN GAMBLERS •CASUAL GAMBLERS
•CUTTING DOWN
•STOPPERS AND STARTERS •SECRET GAMBLERS

Gamblers, like smokers, fall into many categories, but when you examine their reasons for gambling, it becomes apparent that they're all hooked in the same way.

Different people take different approaches to gambling. The gambling industry makes its products available in such a variety of forms and environments that its captive market falls into a wide array of categories.

Different games
- Casino games
- Sports contests
- Lotteries
- Scratch cards
- Bingo
- Slot machines
- Fixed odds betting terminals

- Quiz machines
- Random occurrences, e.g. a white Christmas

Different places
- Casino
- Betting shop
- Sports stadium
- Local shop
- Amusement arcade
- Private party
- At home
- Actually ANYWHERE now that you can gamble from your phone

We tend to have preconceived ideas about what constitutes gambling and which forms are more serious than others. Ask anybody for their definition of a gambler and they're more likely to describe someone who spends their life in the betting shop, race track, or at the casino than someone who buys a ticket for the national lottery each week.

Of course, we know that a huge amount of problem gambling now takes place at home and this has been responsible for a massive increase in the number of women who gamble.

WOMEN GAMBLERS

Not so long ago, women gamblers made up a tiny proportion of the total gambling population. Was this because women were less susceptible to the temptation to gamble, or was it that they lacked the opportunity because of social conventions, which frowned on women spending their time in betting shops and other gambling environments, particularly on their own?

The evidence of recent years answers that question unequivocally. The availability of gambling on the internet has given women the opportunity to gamble without worrying that they might be seen, and they have taken that opportunity in alarming numbers. A recent survey in Britain showed that the number of women who gamble rose by six per cent in just three years. That's approximately half a million women per year taking up gambling for the first time. At 71 per cent of the adult female population, this puts women gamblers almost on a par with men.

If you're one of this burgeoning population of women gamblers, the first thing you must know is that, I'm afraid, you have no excuse for gambling 'because you're a woman'. The fact that so many women are falling into the gambling trap has no more to do with female fallibility than the fact that relatively few women used to gamble was due to female fortitude. What has changed is the role of women in society, the access they now have to gambling, and the way in which the gambling industry has been mercilessly targeting them.

Not only has the shift towards gender equality seen women taking up the vices of men, such as smoking, drinking and gambling, in much greater numbers, but Big Gambling has also spent millions boosting the size of its market by targeting women with the message that gambling is glamorous, sexy and fun, and a good way to unwind.

And women need to unwind now more than ever, because, while there has been a change in expectations about women going out to work, there has yet to be a matching change in expectations about men sharing the workload at home. Consequently, a lot of women find themselves under unrelenting pressure, day in, day out.

IN HER OWN WORDS: ALICE

My daily routine had been getting me down for a while. I'm 40 and I have three children under 10. I wake up early, make breakfast for the kids and prepare their lunches for school. I have to make sure they're dressed properly, their homework is done and they have all they need. Once they've gone, I catch the bus to work to be in by 9am. I work through lunch so I can leave early to pick the kids up from after-school club at 5pm when I take them home and make their tea. Then it's time to prepare dinner for my husband and me. By 9pm I've just about got everyone fed, the kids ready for bed and all their needs taken care of.

I like to keep on top of the washing and ironing, so I'll spend about half an hour on that while my husband washes up. By 10pm I'm exhausted and all I can think about is doing it all again the next day. I need to relax and

I need an escape. That's why I first started gambling. It was easy, it was a change from my routine and it got me off my feet at last. I could also do it in private, without anyone else having to know.

The trouble was, I became so fixated on my daily escape into the world of online gambling that every night I'd want to sit down at the computer and start playing earlier and earlier. I began to put off my main chores, thinking I owed it to myself to give myself a break, and before long I found I was losing my grip. But the one thing I couldn't put off was my daily gambling session. If I'd won the day before, I'd be eager to get back and win more. If I'd lost, I couldn't wait to try and win it back. Either way I was completely hooked.

Even though it was hard being a working mum, I used to take pleasure and pride in getting the kids ready and seeing them go off to school, all neat and tidy and well looked after. After I got hooked on gambling, I started seeing my life as nothing but an endless round of chores. I couldn't see the pleasure in it, only the drudgery. The kids were a nuisance, a burden. The only meaningful thing as far as I could see was my little secret night-time gambling sessions.

Even so, I thought I had it under control and that nobody suspected what I was up to. But kids aren't stupid and nor is my husband. They noticed the change in my behaviour and soon the difficult questions started. I denied it for a while but I couldn't keep lying to them for long particularly as my husband started to notice I was getting through a lot more money and I'd started making up excuses. It was a huge relief when I came clean. I almost wanted to be found out because I felt that it would force me to confront the problem. It was making me irritable, stressed and unwell and I dearly wanted to be rid of it. Fortunately, I got the help I needed from Allen Carr's Easyway before I caused any irreparable damage.

It's easy to understand why Alice turned to gambling. She wanted something to relieve her stress and an escape from her daily routine. Gambling seemed to fit the bill. As long as she was sensible and didn't spend beyond her means, what harm could it do?

Ironically, for Alice gambling didn't provide an escape from her daily routine, it *became* her daily routine and everything she'd considered important before began to suffer as a result. At the same time, it didn't relieve her stress, it caused her much more stress. Remember, addiction causes us to seek relief from stress in the very thing that's causing us stress. It's a vicious circle.

Once she was in the trap, Alice had no control over her gambling. As a result, she gambled beyond her means, causing her even more stress. In addition, she felt more pressure than ever to conceal her gambling from her husband, which increased her stress still further. Her life was becoming miserable and she believed the only time that she could be happy was when she turned on her computer and started gambling.

Alice had set out believing that she could gamble now and then, just as a bit of entertainment and a break from her routine. She quickly found that she was completely hooked.

CASUAL OR OCCASIONAL GAMBLERS

In these times when we're constantly bombarded with ever-changing messages about what's good for us and what's bad, there's one old adage that is always music to our ears.

'A little of what you fancy does you good.'

What this means is that it's safe for you to indulge in anything that might be bad for you, provided you don't do it to excess. While I can accept that a cream cake once in a while won't kill you, I can't see how exactly it does you good. The same is certainly true of smoking and other drugs. Would you say to someone you care about, 'Try a shot of heroin, just a little won't kill you'?

There are two main reasons why ex-gamblers get hooked again. One is that they never completely removed the brainwashing, and so there remains a lingering sense of deprivation. The other is that they reach a point where they're so confident they've overcome their addiction that they decide they can have the occasional gamble without getting hooked again.

Any gambler who has tried to cut down knows that restricting the amount you gamble will only work for a limited period at best. Yet despite knowing this from experience, some gamblers still get hooked again because they believe that they can control their gambling. It's the same delusion that leads people to start gambling in the first place. Be clear about this:

THERE'S NO SUCH THING AS 'JUST ONE BET'

Heavy gamblers wish they could gamble less and, therefore, they envy occasional or casual gamblers who appear to be in control, enjoying the occasional flutter but gambling so infrequently as to avoid getting into trouble. This is an illusion.

NO GAMBLER IS IN CONTROL

ENJOYMENT DOESN'T ENTER INTO IT

Let's get rid of these illusions about occasional gambling once and for all. It's time to explode the myth of the happy, casual gambler. True, some people do not get hooked when they try gambling. They're the lucky ones. But you don't envy them for the limited amount of gambling they do; you envy them for all the gambling they don't do. What is the point in that first bet? If you're lucky you remain a non-gambler; if you're unlucky you get hooked. Heads you gain nothing. Tails you lose everything!

Perhaps you believe there's an idyllic alternative to being either a non-gambler or a gambler who's hooked. A third way: the happy casual gambler. In that case, let me ask you a simple question: why are you not one already? And if you claim to be one, why are you reading this book? Let's establish whether you really want to be a casual gambler.

If I said I could fix it so that you could gamble just once a week for the rest of your life, would you accept it? Better still, suppose I told you that you could control your gambling, so that you did it only when you really wanted to? That's a pretty exciting offer, isn't it? But that's what you already do! Has anyone ever forced you to gamble? Every time you've gambled you've done so because you wanted to, even though part of your brain wished you didn't.

So I take it that you'll settle for just the one gamble a week. Well, if that's what you want, you can do just that. Who's to stop you? In fact, why didn't you just gamble once a week for the whole of your gambling life? Could it be that you wouldn't have been happy gambling just once a week? Of course you wouldn't. Nor would any other gambler.

Sure, there are gamblers who can keep themselves to just one bet a week, but can you really believe that any of them are happy restricting themselves every day, battling the urge to gamble more, for the whole of their lives?

THE TENDENCY IS TO GAMBLE MORE, NOT LESS

There are many external forces that restrict the amount you can gamble: you may have no money and no means to get any; you may be in a place where gambling is forbidden; you may be going through a period when the ill effects of your gambling have become so bad that you're trying to cut down; you may be a secret gambler. Any of these factors will prevent you from gambling whenever you want to.

If all the restrictions were removed, most gamblers would become heavy gamblers relatively quickly.

CUTTING DOWN

Cutting down is really another form of casual gambling. All it does is make each occasion when we do gamble seem more precious, and weaken our motivation to quit. Result: we become more committed gamblers, not more casual ones.

Many gamblers try to cut down in the hope that they can gradually quit that way. All they achieve is to make themselves more miserable than ever and more convinced that they can't live without it. The vast majority of attempts to cut down end up with the gambler betting more and more often.

My question to the casual gambler is this: 'What's the point in gambling at all? Do you think you're getting some genuine pleasure or crutch from those occasions when you gamble? If so, why wait so long in between?'

Most casual gamblers suppress the urge to gamble more. They're still labouring under the illusion that gambling is an escape and a relief, and so when their lives become more stressful, they can quickly turn into heavier gamblers.

YOU MIGHT THINK IT SOUNDS NICE TO WANT TO GAMBLE ONLY EVERY NOW AND THEN. WOULDN'T IT BE NICER NEVER TO WANT TO DO IT AT ALL?

The fact is that these casual gamblers are creating a number of serious problems for themselves:

1. They keep themselves addicted to gambling.

2. They wish their lives away waiting for the next fix.

3. Instead of feeding their addiction whenever they feel like it, they force themselves to starve it, and so are permanently restless.

4. They reinforce the illusion that gambling is precious and enjoyable.

Heavy gamblers eventually lose even the illusion of pleasure. Each coin they put in the slot or chip they toss on to the table becomes automatic and hardly registers on their consciousness. If you watch these heavy gamblers, they show no sign of enjoying what they're doing. In fact they look so bored with the monotony that they seem barely alive. You'll find that the occasions when you relish gambling most always occur after a period of abstinence. This is because there's no genuine pleasure or crutch whatsoever in gambling purely for gambling's sake. All that gamblers enjoy is the temporary relief from the aggravation caused by the craving for the next bet.

Cutting down increases the illusion of pleasure because the longer you endure the craving, the greater the pleasure seems when you relieve that craving.

If you think increasing the illusion of pleasure sounds like a good thing, think again. The only way to increase the illusion of pleasure is to increase the aggravation. It's like wearing tighter and tighter shoes in order to get increasing relief by taking them off. No gambler, including casual gamblers, enjoys the aggravation of being a gambler. There's a constant impulse to scratch an itch, and the more you scratch it, the worse it gets.

That's why cutting down is unsustainable and usually results in gambling more than before.

STOPPERS AND STARTERS

Heavy gamblers think that casual gamblers have the best of all possible worlds, but it's an illusion. They neither gamble whenever they want to, nor do they have the marvellous joy of being free. The same is true of stoppers and starters, another breed of gambler often envied by heavy gamblers.

These aren't strictly casual gamblers, but tend to be regarded in the same light. In fact, quite often they're very heavy gamblers, but rather than being seen as poor fools who keep falling back into the same trap, they're regarded as lucky people who have the enviable ability to stop gambling and start again whenever they choose. Of course, they don't like to appear stupid any more than the rest of us, so they tend to encourage the misconception. Be clear about this: it's a lie.

Look at the situation logically. Why do these people keep stopping? For the same reason that any other gambler does: they don't enjoy being gamblers.

Having become non-gamblers, why do they change their mind and decide to become gamblers again? There can be only one answer to that: they don't enjoy being non-gamblers either.

What tragic people! Neither happy as gamblers nor as non-gamblers: the worst of all worlds. When they're gambling, they envy non-gamblers. They go through the trauma of stopping using the willpower method, but never become happy non-gamblers, so they start again. Then they remember why they stopped in the first place. They're permanently miserable.

Remember, to be a happy non-gambler for the rest of your life, you need to achieve the right frame of mind. If you believe that there's some genuine pleasure or benefit in gambling, you might never gamble again, but you'll suffer a feeling of deprivation and will remain vulnerable for the rest of your life. If you want to gamble once, what will prevent you from wanting to gamble again and again and again?

You may think, 'If Easyway makes it easy to quit, what possible danger can there be in gambling now and then? Even if I do get hooked again, I can just use the method to quit again.' If you have a desire to continue gambling at all, you haven't understood Easyway.

The whole object of this method is to remove your desire to

gamble altogether, because if you want to do it just once, you'll want to do it again and again. Even if you don't actually gamble but you still feel the desire, you will not be a happy non-gambler. You will feel deprived. You will be a miserable ex-gambler. Which brings us to the most miserable gamblers of all.

SECRET GAMBLERS

Secret gamblers spend their lives living a lie. Not only do they lie to themselves that they get some pleasure or crutch from gambling, they also lie to the people they love that they're not gamblers at all! They're so utterly ashamed of what they are that they don't want other people to know.

To break a solemn promise to someone that you love and trust is bad enough, but then to compound that by lying in order to cover up your failure is the ultimate humiliation. Many otherwise honest people are reduced to this because of gambling.

If you gamble openly you can at least stand up and claim that you do so because you choose to. As a secret gambler, you can't even adopt that brazen attitude of self-delusion. You have to admit to yourself that you're a pathetic slave. You go through life despising yourself. Remember the pitcher plant on page 77. All the various types of gambler that I've described in this chapter – heavy or casual gamblers, stoppers and starters and secret gamblers – they're all in the same trap.

DON'T ENVY ANY OF THEM

SUMMARY

• The addiction to gambling is the same whether you're a man or a woman.

• The tendency is to gamble more and more.

• Casual gamblers are never fulfilled either.

• Cutting down doesn't work.

• Stoppers and starters are never happy.

• Secret gamblers are the most miserable of all.

Chapter 14

NOTHING TO FEAR

IN THIS CHAPTER
- *WHAT YOU'VE ACHIEVED SO FAR*
- *TIME TO MAKE A NEW CHOICE*
- *KNOW YOUR ENEMY*

In order to achieve the certainty required to quit gambling easily and permanently, you need to remove the fear of stopping. Approach the subject with an open mind and try to be relaxed, logical and rational. Then your fears will dissolve.

In Chapter 1, I explained how Easyway works like the combination to open a safe. In order to use the combination successfully you need to know all the numbers and apply them in order. You may have found that information frustrating at the time. You were eager to discover the solution to your gambling problem and the prospect of reading through the whole book may have seemed daunting.

But you persevered and now you stand on the brink of becoming a happy non-gambler. You've come a long way towards achieving the state of mind necessary for you to quit and remain free for the rest of your life.

Congratulate yourself on your achievements. Remind yourself

that there's no need to feel miserable; on the contrary, you have every reason to feel excited. You're releasing yourself from a prison that has brought you nothing but stress and misery and you're choosing a life that will bring you more happiness than you can imagine.

Perhaps you think you have no reason to congratulate yourself. The effects of your gambling problem are still there, your debts haven't got any smaller, your lifestyle hasn't changed and you're still struggling to convince yourself that this is going to be as easy as I say.

SEEING THE REAL PICTURE

In the context of stopping gambling, the fear of success is caused by illusions. These illusions have been put in your brain by many influences, each of which has a vested interest in you continuing to gamble. You've been brainwashed into believing that gambling is sexy, exciting, enjoyable and makes you happy, when the reality is the complete opposite.

You also fear that stopping will be hard, maybe too hard to bear. You fell into the gambling trap easily but assume that it will be incredibly difficult to climb out, as if the trap were a hole in the ground covered with branches and leaves into which you stumbled unwittingly and now find yourself in over your head.

But that's not the case. Though it may feel like a deep, dark hole, there's no physical effort required to escape. You simply need to make a choice. It's a simple choice between taking a step backwards or a step forward. You can either choose to remain in the gambling trap for the rest of your life, going deeper and deeper into it, becoming poorer and poorer and more and more enslaved and miserable, or you can choose freedom.

You were lured into the gambling trap by the illusions peddled to you by people with a vested interest in you giving them your money. You took a step backwards. And you've found that it makes you miserable. So now you just have to choose to do the opposite. Take a step forwards. It's as simple as that. However, perhaps you still have fears.

Some of our fears are instinctive. For example, the fear of heights or the fear of fire are instinctive responses that protect us from falling or getting burnt. There's nothing instinctive about the fear of getting out of the gambling trap.

THE FEAR OF STOPPING GAMBLING IS BASED ON ILLUSIONS

IT'S YOUR DECISION

Once you're free from gambling, you'll be amazed at how easy it was to escape. You'll lead a far happier life and your only regret will be not having made your escape sooner.

At the moment you may still feel trapped and unable to see a way out. But once you do get out, you'll realise that all you had to do was take a step forward instead of a step back. It's as simple as that.

In order to achieve success you need to remove all doubt.

You must understand and accept that your fears of trying to live without gambling are based on illusions. In reality, you have nothing to fear.

Perhaps you question whether it's possible to know for certain that something will *not* happen, i.e. even if you do manage to quit gambling, how do you know you won't fall into the trap again? After all, the chances of being struck by a meteorite are infinitesimally small, yet nobody can say with absolute certainty that it'll never happen to them.

That's true. However, you have a considerable advantage over potential meteorite victims. If a meteorite is going to hit you, there's nothing you can do about it, whereas only you can make yourself go back to gambling. You're in control and once you've seen through the confidence trick that kept you in the gambling trap, you'll never be taken in again.

If you still have doubts and fears at this stage, don't worry, that's perfectly normal. You've been brainwashed into thinking you have to make huge sacrifices to become a non-gambler; that the process will be hard and miserable; and that, even if you do succeed, you'll forever be tempted to gamble again. These are illusions. Once the brainwashing has been removed, you will be in the right frame of mind and your fears will evaporate.

My second instruction was to keep an open mind. If you've done that, you'll realise by now that the fears you had about stopping gambling were mere illusions, and so they were without foundation.

If you're unclear on this point, I urge you to go back and

read Chapter 5 through again, making sure you allow your mind to take it all on board. In order to undo the brainwashing, you need to accept that you've been brainwashed and understand how that brainwashing has distorted your perceptions. Then you can see things as they really are.

Remember the STOP diagram in Chapter 6? If I hadn't told you that there was a message there, you would never have been able to see it. But as soon as I told you about the message and how to see it, you quickly did. And once you'd seen it, you couldn't fail to see it every time.

ONCE YOU SEE THINGS AS THEY REALLY ARE, YOU CAN NEVER BE FOOLED AGAIN

NO GET-OUT CLAUSE

Some gamblers try to allay their fear of stopping by telling themselves they can always start again if it gets too hard – that quitting doesn't have to be final.

If you start off with that attitude, you're very likely to fail sooner or later. Instead, start off with the certainty that you're going to be free forever. To achieve that certainty, you have to remove the fear and panic first.

TIME TO TAKE CONTROL

You've already come a long way in the process of unravelling the brainwashing that has kept you in the gambling trap and putting yourself in the right frame of mind to escape. Now you're going to start taking the practical forward steps that will see you become a happy non-gambler for the rest of your life.

Your first positive step was choosing to read this book. You had a choice: to bury your head in the sand and continue stumbling further and further into the miserable slavery of gambling, or to take positive action to resolve the situation. You made a positive choice. All I ask is that you continue making positive choices.

As we move forward, there are three very important facts that I want you to remember:

1. Gambling does absolutely nothing for you at all.
It's crucial that you understand why this is so and accept it, so that you never get a feeling of deprivation.

2. There's no need for a transitional period.
With drug addicts this is often referred to as the 'withdrawal period'. But anyone who quits with Easyway has no need to worry about the withdrawal period. Yes, it may take time to repair the damage caused by your gambling problem, but the moment you stop gambling is the moment you become free. You don't have to wait for anything to happen.

3. There's no such thing as 'just this once' or 'the occasional flutter'.
Just one bet is enough to make you a gambler again and must be seen for what it is: part of a lifelong chain of self-destruction.

PRACTICAL STEPS

Take a pen and paper and write down all the activities that used to give you the most pleasure before you became addicted to gambling. Really think about it. Take a day or two over it if you like and write down the things you enjoyed as they come to mind. Focus on the times when you felt most relaxed and happy, and when gambling was furthest from your mind. This will help you to become aware of what you really enjoy and value in life. Your list might look something like this:

Seeing friends

Going for a walk

Going for a bike ride

Having a nice meal

Reading

Going to the cinema

Doing or watching sport

Gardening

Listening to music

Having a Saturday morning lie-in

Planning activities with your partner or children

KNOW YOUR ENEMY

Many addicts suffer the illusion that they can never get completely free. They convince themselves that their addiction is their friend, their source of confidence, their crutch, even part of their identity. And so they fear that if they quit, they will not only lose their closest companion, they will lose a part of themselves.

That anyone should come to regard something that is destroying them and making them miserable as a friend is a stark indication of just how severely the brainwashing distorts reality.

When you lose a friend, you grieve. Eventually you come to terms with the loss and life goes on, but you're left with a genuine void in your life that you can never fill. There's nothing you can do about it. You've no choice but to accept the situation and, though it still hurts, you do.

When gamblers, smokers, alcoholics, heroin and other addicts try to quit by willpower, they feel they're losing a friend. They know that they're making the right decision to stop, but they still suffer a feeling of sacrifice and, therefore, there's a void in their lives. It isn't a genuine void, but they believe it is and so the effect is the same. They feel as if they're mourning for a friend. Yet this false friend isn't even dead. The purveyors of drugs and gambling make absolutely sure that these tortured souls are forever subjected to the temptation of forbidden fruit for the rest of their lives.

However, when you rid yourself of your mortal enemy, in this case gambling, there's no need to mourn. On the contrary, you can rejoice and celebrate from the start, and you can continue to rejoice and celebrate for the rest of your life. You're not losing a friend, you're getting rid of an enemy.

> I love blackjack. But I'm not addicted to gambling. I'm addicted to sitting in a semicircle.
>
> **Mitch Hedberg (comedian)**

That's why it's vital to get it clear in your mind that gambling isn't your friend, nor is it part of your identity. It never has been. In fact, it's your mortal enemy and by getting rid of it you're sacrificing nothing, just making marvellous, positive gains.

So the answer to the question, 'When will I be free?' is, 'Whenever you choose to be.'

You could spend the next few days, and possibly the rest of your life, continuing to believe that gambling was your friend and wondering when you'll stop missing it. If you do that, you'll feel miserable, the desire to gamble may never leave you and you'll either end up feeling deprived for the rest of your life, or you'll end up going back to gambling and feeling even worse.

Alternatively, you can recognise gambling for the mortal enemy that it really is and take pleasure in cutting it out of your life. Then you need never crave it again and whenever it enters your mind you'll feel elated that it's no longer ruining your life and you'll have a wonderful feeling of freedom.

Unlike people who quit with the willpower method, you'll be happy to think about your old enemy and you needn't try to block it from your mind. In fact, it's important that you don't. Trying not to think about something is a sure way of becoming obsessed with it. If I tell you not to think about elephants, what's the first thing that comes into your head? Exactly!

There's no reason to try not to think about gambling, but it is important to think about it in the right way: you need to replace the illusions of gambling with the reality of having your life dominated by this awful addiction. Enjoy thinking about it and rejoice that you're free.

REPROGRAMME YOUR BRAIN

I asked you to approach this process with a relaxed, rational and open mind, because that helps you understand the gambling trap and the Little Monster that complains when you don't feed your urge to gamble. During the first few days after your final bet, the Little Monster will be grumbling away, sending messages to your brain that it wants you to interpret as, 'I want to gamble'.

But you now understand the true picture and, instead of gambling, or getting into a panic because you can't gamble, pause for a moment. Take a deep breath. There's nothing to fear. There's no pain. The feeling isn't bad. It's what gamblers suffer throughout their gambling lives.

In the past, your mind interpreted the pangs of the Little Monster as 'I want to gamble' because it had every reason to believe that gambling would satisfy the empty, insecure feeling. But now you understand that, far from relieving that feeling, gambling causes it. So just relax, accept the feeling for what it really is – the death throes of the Little Monster – and remind yourself, 'Non-gamblers don't have this problem. This is what gamblers suffer and they suffer it throughout their gambling lives. It's great to be free!'

THE WITHDRAWAL PANGS WILL THEN CEASE TO FEEL LIKE PANGS AND WILL BECOME MOMENTS OF PLEASURE

You might find that, particularly during the first few days, you forget that you've quit. It can happen at any time. You think, 'I'll go and have a bet.' Then you remember you're now a non-gambler. You wonder why the thought entered your head when you were convinced you'd reversed the brainwashing. Such times can be crucial in whether you succeed or not. React in the wrong way and they can be disastrous. Doubts can surface and you may start to question your decision to quit and lose faith in yourself. React in the right way and they can act as confirmation that you really have kicked it.

Don't worry about these situations. Just remain calm and, instead of thinking, 'I can't or I mustn't do it,' think, 'Isn't it great? I don't need to do that anymore. I'm free!'

The mental associations between certain everyday things such as sport and gambling can linger on after the Little Monster has died and this undermines the attempts of gamblers who quit with the willpower method.

In their minds they've built up a massive case against gambling, they've decided to become a non-gambler, they've managed to go for however long without gambling and yet on certain occasions a voice keeps saying, 'I want to gamble.' They haven't killed the Big Monster and so they still think of gambling as a pleasure or crutch.

Although you'll no longer suffer the illusion that you're being deprived, it's still imperative that you prepare yourself for these situations. If you momentarily forget that you no longer gamble, that isn't a bad sign, it's a good one. It's proof that your life is returning to the happy state you were in before you got hooked on gambling, when it didn't dominate your whole existence.

Expecting these moments to happen and being prepared for them means you won't be caught off guard. You'll be wearing a suit of impregnable armour. You know you've made the correct decision and nobody will be able to make you doubt it. That way, instead of being the cause of your downfall, these moments can give you strength, security and immense pleasure, reminding you just how wonderful it is to be

FREE!

SUMMARY

- Gambling isn't a hole in the ground – there's no physical effort required to get out.

- It's easy to walk free – you just have to make a different choice.

- Have no doubts about the choice you're making – you know it's the right one.

- Remember, gambling does nothing for you at all.

- There's nothing to wait for. The moment you stop gambling is the moment you become free.

- There's no such thing as 'the occasional flutter'. All gambling is part of a chain of misery.

- Rejoice at ridding yourself of your mortal enemy.

Chapter 15

TAKING CONTROL

IN THIS CHAPTER
- *FREE YOURSELF*
- *WHAT WILL HAPPEN IF YOU DON'T*
- *ENJOY THE THRILL OF GETTING YOUR LIFE BACK*

Gamblers hate the confusion of sensing that they're not in control. Taking control is easy when you base your choices on facts not illusions.

Although we are constantly bombarded by misinformation designed to make us gamble, all gamblers are aware of the many good reasons not to. The frequent attempts to stop or cut down are driven by one or more of these reasons, but it's only when you succeed in stopping that you realise the greatest gain is to escape from slavery.

Gamblers don't like to think of themselves as slaves. Heavy gamblers tend to be strong-willed people who have enjoyed a high degree of control over most of their lives and they find it particularly frustrating to have to admit that gambling is controlling them. They believe they should be able to conquer their problem through sheer force of will and, when they can't, it leaves them feeling frustrated, depressed and short-tempered.

Some gamblers are so fearful of stopping that they go to great lengths to shut out from their lives anyone or anything that might pressurise them to do so and close their minds to the terrible effects of being a gambler. Though they know and hate the fact that they're not in control, they refuse to confront the most severe and misery-inducing effect of all: the sheer slavery.

Money is the most common reason gamblers give for wanting to quit. Throwing away thousands of pounds that you cannot afford is always going to lead to severe stress and misery, and the average gambler can expect to lose around £50,000 in their lifetime. You may be reading that figure wishing, 'If only it was that little!' However much money you've already wasted on gambling, the really good news is that very soon you'll never have to throw away another penny. How marvellous to be free to spend your money on things that will bring genuine pleasure to you and those around you rather than being forced to squander it on something you wish you didn't do!

The social effects of gambling are also a common reason for wanting to quit. The effect that gambling addiction has on your moods and behaviour, and how that affects family and friends, can be devastating and if you're fortunate enough to quit before it's too late, then you can avoid the additional misery of seeing your relationships disintegrate irretrievably.

However, the money and the chance to rebuild your relationships with friends and family should not be your main motivation. If they were motivation enough, you'd already be free. I want you to stop gambling for one reason and one reason alone: the purely selfish fact that you'll enjoy your life so much more as a non-gambler. The money, the relationships, the return of your self-esteem, the fact that you'll be less stressed, more relaxed and happier are all wonderful bonuses to enjoy when you achieve what you have set out to achieve: TO BE FREE.

Ask a gambler why they gamble and they'll nearly always react defensively and negatively. They can't seem to find reasons why they do, but resort to excuses for why they haven't been able to stop.

'I can afford it.'

'I make sure it doesn't affect my family.'

'It's my only vice.'

Defensiveness is a sure sign of someone who knows they're not in control. The key that will enable you to get free is the realisation that you no longer need to be a slave to gambling; that you'll enjoy life more; that you'll be able to deal better with stress; and that far from having to go through some terrible trauma in order to escape, you'll be a happy non-gambler right from the moment you make your decision to stop and, most importantly of all, YOU WILL NOT MISS IT.

You'll look back on your days as a gambler and rejoice in your newfound freedom. The freedom to look upon other gamblers, not with envy or deprivation, but with genuine pity, just as you would look upon a heroin addict. The greatest gain to be made from becoming a non-gambler isn't so much the money or the stability – although they're fantastic bonuses – but no longer having to despise yourself for being a slave. It's a freedom that all gamblers wish they could enjoy.

One of the ingenious illusions of the gambling trap is that you're in control of what you're doing because you weigh up the odds, study the form, size up the opposition, examine the conditions and then seize the moment.

The truth is that the odds are always loaded against you and the only decision that really matters is whether you gamble or not.

Funnily enough, when it comes to this decision, gamblers become aware that they're not, in fact, in control. They're very familiar with all the powerful reasons not to gamble, yet they feel powerless to resist the urge.

When you first start gambling, the feeling of control is strong. Your wins strengthen your belief that you know what you're doing, while your losses are dismissed because at this stage they're small enough not to be a threat to your way of life.

However, as you slide further into the trap, the stakes get higher and your feeling of control diminishes. Now you're risking amounts of money at a frequency that you know will have an impact on your way of life. Perhaps it will force you to lie to people who trust you, or compel you to sell something precious, or make you deny something important to a loved one. You know that you're taking a dreadful risk by gambling, yet you go ahead and do it anyway.

This conflict creates a feeling of self-loathing, which is often expressed as irritability towards others. When you're in the gambling trap, you're pulled in opposite directions. Part of your brain is telling you not to gamble, but another part is demanding that you do. It leaves you in a state of anxiety and confusion: if you want to stop, why can't you just stop? With other things in life, you know that if you wanted to stop and had very good reasons to do so, you would immediately, so why can't you apply the same control with gambling?

The answer is clear: you're not in control. There's a force controlling you, compelling you to make choices that go against your instincts. That force has a name:

ADDICTION

Gamblers believe they choose to gamble, after all nobody's holding a gun to their head. Surely every time you place a bet, you're exercising your own personal choice? But are you in reality? You're reading this book because you want to stop. If you had the choice, you would therefore choose not to gamble. Addiction involves the removal of choice.

This constant battle between the desire to stop and the compulsion to continue goes on in every addict's mind. It's confusing and makes us feel foolish and pathetic. Nobody likes to feel that way, so we go into denial; we bury our head in the sand to try to avoid the painful truth about what we've become: a hopeless, pathetic slave to gambling. Instead of facing up to this unpleasant reality and doing the one thing that will free us – stop gambling – we search for excuses to continue.

We delude ourselves that if we got into this mess through gambling, we ought to be able to get ourselves out of it in the same way. We still hope desperately that we can regain control and use gambling to restore everything we've lost. The more we convince ourselves that gambling is the answer to our problem, the more addicted we become, and the more we lose. We find ourselves in a truly bizarre situation: believing that gambling is both the problem and the solution to that problem.

Only when you face up to your situation and admit that you've lost control can you escape from the trap. In order to take control, you have to recognise and understand that gambling controls you, not the other way round, and that gambling isn't the solution to your misery but the cause.

Once you've quit and are enjoying life again and coping better with stress, you'll no longer have to block your mind to the terrible consequences of gambling. On the contrary, one of the huge bonuses of quitting is that you'll no longer need to worry about them.

CUT YOUR LOSSES

Most gamblers see their situation as an ongoing game. At any given time, they may be up or they may be down, but the game isn't over. How many times have you won money, only to blow it all again?

As singer Gladys Knight said,

WINNING IS THE WORST THING THAT CAN HAPPEN TO A GAMBLER

Winning keeps you more firmly trapped than losing. It reinforces the illusion of pleasure and the illusion of control. When we win we put it down to skill, when we lose we blame bad luck.

When you lose, it's easier to see the negative effects that gambling has. Even so, the last thing you want to do when you're down is walk away. Even when our losses are catastrophic, we regard them as part of an ongoing game and we kid ourselves that if we keep playing we have the chance to win it all back. Such is our fear of life without gambling that stopping seems unthinkable.

'If I stop while I'm down, everyone will know I'm a loser. They'll want to know where the money's gone and I'll have to admit the truth.'

'All I need is a few breaks and I can put my life back together again. I just need my luck to change.'

'I've invested so much time and money, I can't walk away now with nothing to show for it.'

The fear of being found out; the shame of wasting all that time and money, not to mention the emotional investment, and having nothing to show for it; the misguided belief that gambling could still provide your escape: these are all common among gambling addicts. Non-gamblers don't suffer these feelings. They're caused by gambling. As long as you believe that any one of them is a reason to keep gambling, you'll continue to slide deeper and deeper into the trap, like the fly in the pitcher plant.

Unlike the fly, you have one distinct advantage. Once the fly is on the slippery slope, escape is impossible. You, on the other hand, can escape any time you choose. You simply need to see through the brainwashing, remove the illusions that create the desire to gamble and STOP. Only by stopping can you take control.

The more you gamble, the more desperate your situation becomes. Once your own money runs out, you turn to friends or family for loans. You don't want them to know that you need the money for gambling, so you lie about your reasons for borrowing. When you lose that money and can't pay it back, you have to find someone else to borrow from. Pretty soon all your options are exhausted. You know you're in a desperate situation but you tell yourself that you can solve it all if only you could get a few breaks.

> *One of the worst things that can happen to you in life is to win a bet at an early age.*
>
> **Danny McGoorty (pool room hustler)**

Your luck has to change soon, but you need to find some more money from somewhere. What have you gone without to fund your gambling? What have your loved ones gone without? It's no surprise that a high percentage of problem gamblers end up committing crimes to fund their addiction. In many cases these crimes are committed against people they're close to: friends, family, business colleagues. This has a devastating effect on your self-esteem and the fear of being found out puts you under terrific stress. Your health suffers, you find it hard to concentrate at work, you have no time for your loved ones and you lose the ability to enjoy the real pleasures in life.

Millions of people all over the world know how this feels.

And yet they suffer it alone. The terror of having to face all those people they've lied to and stolen from makes gamblers do everything they can to conceal their predicament and that often means suffering in silence.

It's a tragic situation with a tragic ending. The gambler looks in the mirror and sees a slave, a liar, a thief and a loner. The realisation that the situation has gone way beyond your control can be devastating. We know we can't pull the wool over people's eyes any more and that our pathetic, shameful situation is going to be laid bare. The tragic fact is that some people choose the only alternative they can see: suicide.

I am not trying to shock you into stopping. I merely want to point out what you're letting yourself in for if you continue to allow yourself to be controlled by gambling. You're in a prison and there's no way out through gambling, there's only deeper despair. But fortunately there is an easy way to escape.

It's time to see your situation as it really is. Each bet merely pushes you further into the trap. It's time to take control. It's time to STOP.

ENJOY BREAKING FREE

Remember, your fear isn't relieved by gambling, it's caused by it. You've nothing to fear from stopping, there are only marvellous gains to be made. Think about the fly in the pitcher plant. You could set it free by encouraging it to fly out while it still has the chance. This book is doing the equivalent for you. Think about how a non-gambler sees you. They see all the harm that gambling is causing you and think, 'Why don't you just stop? Then you'll no longer have the problem.'

It's the same thing we all think when we see a heroin addict. It's obvious that each time they inject the drug into a vein they're not curing their problem but making it worse. The only thing that will end the problem for them is to stop taking heroin.

> There is no magical formula to beat the casino. None. Save your money.
> **John-Talmage Mathis**
> **(writer)**

This is your chance to fly free. In fact, you can fly free any time you choose, so why wait?

You have nothing to fear. Remember, misery and degradation are guaranteed as long as you stay in the gambling trap. Escape and you can take control of putting your life back together. You'll be amazed by how good it feels to be free from the slavery of gambling. The benefits are enormous:

- More self-respect

- More time for work and play

- A greater ability to concentrate

- A greater ability to cope with stress

• Being able to enjoy genuine pleasures again

• A healthier lifestyle

• A sharper, brighter, happier state of mind

• Real control over your life

• Relationships rebuilt

• Ending the loneliness

• More confidence

• More money

• More freedom.

Your moment to take control and escape from the gambling trap has arrived. Congratulations! You should be feeling excited.

ENJOY THE PROCESS OF ESCAPE. LOOK FORWARD TO ALL THE BENEFITS YOU'RE ABOUT TO RECEIVE.

And whenever the thought of gambling enters your mind, don't feel miserable because you can't, think, 'YIPPEE! I don't have to do that any more. I'm FREE!'

```
┌-------------------  SUMMARY  ------------------┐
! • It's time to stop being a slave to gambling.         !
! • You don't choose to be a gambler.                    !
! • The only way to regain control is to stop.           !
! • Free yourself and you'll be amazed how good life becomes. !
! • Do it for yourself – everything else is a bonus.     !
└------------------------------------------------┘
```

Chapter 16

WITHDRAWAL

IN THIS CHAPTER
• WITHDRAWAL CAUSES NO PHYSICAL PAIN • THAT PANIC FEELING
• KILLING THE LITTLE MONSTER • WHEN DOES IT END?
• PREPARING FOR YOUR FINAL GAMBLE

When you quit by using Easyway, the withdrawal symptoms become a source of pleasure, not pain.

Just as drug addicts fear that they will have to go through a painful period of withdrawal after they stop and the chemical leaves their body, gamblers also fear that they will not be able to resist the craving.

In fact, the physical withdrawal pangs are so slight that you can hardly feel them. The same is true of the most addictive drug of all: nicotine. We only think the withdrawal is severe because of the trauma people suffer on the willpower method, but that's psychological not physical and completely avoidable with Easyway.

I've explained that the only reason a gambler continues to gamble is to relieve the pangs of withdrawal. So if those pangs are so slight as to be almost imperceptible, why do gamblers find it so difficult to endure the cravings when they quit on willpower?

Let's draw a comparison with smoking. Every night, millions of smokers manage to sleep soundly for eight hours and, when they wake up, they're not in agony after having gone so long without their drug. If the physical withdrawal really were terrible, it would wake them up during the night. But in reality most smokers get up, get dressed and have breakfast before lighting up. Not only are they getting by quite happily without any physical pain, they're not even aware of any discomfort.

The same is true of gamblers. When you wake up in the morning, do you feel in agony because you've gone so long without gambling?

Perhaps you don't expect to feel any physical pain because gambling doesn't involve a substance like nicotine, which causes a reaction in your body. But gambling works in a similar way, creating a chemical change in your brain. When you stop gambling your brain does send out a physical response, which we interpret as 'I want to gamble'.

> The only thing that overcomes hard luck is hard work.
>
> **Harry Golden**
> **(writer and publisher)**

When you wake up in the morning there's no trace of physical pain. Sure, you may look forward to the next time you can gamble again and if someone stood in your way at that point and prevented you from doing so you would probably get very angry, but that's not a reaction to physical pain; it's panic at the thought of being deprived. When you're confident of having your next bet, this panic recedes. If it were a physical pain, it would be there all the time, like toothache.

AVOIDING PANIC

Most gamblers are familiar with the 'panic feeling' that sets in when they don't know when they'll next get the opportunity to gamble. It's like a smoker running out of cigarettes. Smokers will go to great lengths to replenish their supply, often walking through the rain late at night just to stock up on their little 'crutch'. Gamblers too will go to incredible lengths to ensure they're not denied the opportunity to gamble, sneaking out of the house, lying about where they're going and even putting themselves in dangerous situations.

But occasionally you meet a gambler who claims not to know the panic feeling. Not all of them are lying. We know that gamblers lie, to others and to themselves, but there are some who genuinely never feel this panic of not knowing where their next opportunity to bet is going to come from. The simple reason is that they're so frightened of finding themselves in that position that they take every precaution to make sure it never happens!

In other words, far from being less affected by the panic than most gamblers, they're even more consumed by it. The truth is that every gambler who is denied the opportunity to gamble experiences the panic feeling. But remember:

THE WITHDRAWAL FROM GAMBLING CAUSES
NO PHYSICAL PAIN

You may dispute this. Perhaps you've read about withdrawal from gambling and seen lists of the physical effects it can induce. Effects such as:

• Tiredness

• Headaches

• Stomach upsets

• Weak and aching muscles

• Heart palpitations

• The shakes

• The sweats

• The shivers

• Difficult breathing.

This set of symptoms is very similar to the symptoms of flu. No doubt you've had flu on several occasions in your life and you probably expect to get it again, but the thought of doing so doesn't induce panic. Even though flu can make you feel awful, it's not a pain you can't withstand.

In fact, we're very well equipped to deal with pain. Try it for yourself. Squeeze your thigh and, digging your fingernails in, gradually increase the pressure. You'll find you can endure quite a severe level of pain without any sense of fear or panic. That's because you're in control. You know what's causing the pain and you know that you can make it stop whenever you choose.

Now repeat the exercise and, when the pain is as much as you can bear, try to imagine that it wasn't you causing it but that it had just suddenly started and that you knew neither the cause nor how long it would last. Now imagine that pain being in your head or chest. You would immediately panic.

Pain isn't the problem; the problem is the fear and panic that pain induces if you don't understand why you're feeling it or what the consequences might be. In fact, we often panic at the slightest feeling of discomfort if we don't know what's caused it and fear it might be the beginning of something calamitous.

GAMBLERS SUFFER WITHDRAWAL PANGS ALL THE TIME, THAT'S WHAT KEEPS THEM GAMBLING

Observe gamblers, especially when they're denied the opportunity to gamble. They'll be restless and fidgety. You'll notice little nervous tics. They'll constantly be doing things with their hands or grinding their teeth. This restlessness is triggered by an empty, insecure feeling, which can quickly turn into frustration, irritability, anxiety, anger, fear and panic if they're not able to gamble.

Get it clear in your mind that gambling causes this feeling, it doesn't relieve it. As long as you understand that, you don't need to feel deprived when you stop.

IF YOU CONTINUE TO GAMBLE, YOU'LL SUFFER THAT EMPTY, INSECURE FEELING FOR THE REST OF YOUR LIFE

A WILFUL AGONY

The withdrawal symptoms I listed above are what gamblers suffer when they try to quit with the willpower method. Perhaps you've experienced this yourself. They're all symptoms of anxiety, induced by the feeling that they're being deprived of their pleasure or crutch.

The problem is not the physical withdrawal caused by the Little Monster – as mentioned, this is so slight that most gamblers are scarcely even aware of it. The real problem is the way the Little Monster triggers the Big Monster to think, 'I want to gamble,' and if you can't you feel frustrated and miserable, which in turn can cause the symptoms listed previously.

IGNORANCE AND ILLUSION ARE THE TWIN EVILS THAT COMBINE TO TURN A SMALL PHYSICAL SIGNAL INTO PANIC AND MENTAL TORTURE

Imagine having a permanent itch that you were not allowed to scratch. Imagine how that would torment you and think about the amount of willpower you would have to summon up to resist scratching the itch even once. Imagine also that you believed the itch would last for the rest of your life unless you were allowed to scratch it.

How long do you think you could last before you scratched the itch? If you did manage to hold out for a week or even more, imagine the relief you would feel when you finally gave in.

This is the torture that gamblers go through when trying to quit with the willpower method. For them the desire to gamble lasts long after the Little Monster has died, because the Big Monster is still alive, interpreting various triggers as 'I need to gamble'. The Big Monster is aroused by everything they ever associated with gambling, such as watching sport, surfing the internet, feeling depressed or stressed and needing some space. They think, 'I used to gamble on these occasions,' and they still believe they're being deprived.

You must remember that the perception of gambling as a pleasure or crutch is a figment of your imagination, left over from the brainwashing.

I found it easy to stop smoking because I realised that the empty, insecure feeling of wanting a cigarette was caused by the last cigarette I smoked, and that the one thing that would ensure I suffered that feeling for the rest of my life would be to smoke another.

I endured none of the suffering that I had gone through on previous attempts because I realised I was not being deprived. On the contrary, I experienced a wonderful feeling of freedom.

Exactly the same applies to you and gambling. Once you've

accepted that the pleasure or crutch is just an illusion, you will feel no deprivation and, consequently, no misery or torture. Just a wonderful feeling of freedom.

THE PLEASURE OF WITHDRAWAL

After you've made your decision to quit, you might continue to experience a sense of withdrawal for a few days as your brain and body adjust. Remember, this isn't physical pain, it's just the Little Monster demanding to be fed. It's a mild, empty, slightly insecure feeling which can be a little disorientating. However, light though it is, you should not ignore it.

It's essential to keep in mind that the Little Monster was created when you first started gambling and it has continued to feed on every subsequent bet you've made. As soon as you stop gambling, you cut off its food supply and that evil monster begins to die.

In its death throes the Little Monster will try to entice you to feed it. Create a mental image of this parasite getting weaker and weaker and enjoy starving it to death. That way the pangs cease to feel like withdrawal and become moments of pleasure.

Keep this mental image with you at all times and make sure you don't respond to its death throes by thinking, 'I want to gamble.' Remember that the empty, insecure feeling was caused by your last bet. It isn't a pleasant feeling in itself, but you'll enjoy it because you'll understand the cause and know it means that the Little Monster inside you is dying.

Take pleasure and delight in killing off the Little Monster. Even if you do get that feeling of 'I want to gamble' for a few days, don't worry about it. It's just the Little Monster doing everything it can to tempt you to feed it. As long as you see that, you'll find it easy to starve it to death. You now have complete control over it. It's no longer destroying you; you're destroying it and soon you'll be free forever.

WHEN CAN I RELAX?

You're probably thinking, 'OK, but how long before I'm cured?' You can start enjoying the genuine pleasure of being a non-gambler from the moment you make your decision never to gamble again. Unlike the willpower method, with Easyway you don't have to wait for anything.

The time it takes for the chemicals in your brain to return to normal levels can vary, but there's no need to wait. From day one you can get on with life and help the chemical process by engaging in genuine pleasures. People who quit with the willpower method often spend weeks or months feeling completely obsessed with being denied what they see as their pleasure or crutch. Then, there might come a moment when they suddenly realise that they haven't thought about gambling for a while. It's a dangerous moment.

They've gone from believing that life will always be miserable without it, to a point where it hasn't even crossed their mind for a while. They feel great. Surely this is it – they've made it! It's time to celebrate. What possible harm could it do to reward themselves with just one little flutter?

If they're misguided enough to give in to this temptation and place a bet, they will revive the Little Monster who will start demanding that they place another. Panic starts to creep back in. They don't want their efforts to quit to be derailed so easily and for nothing, so they draw on all their willpower and vow not to give in to the urge to gamble again.

But sooner or later they will regain their confidence and will be tempted again, and this time they can say to themselves, 'I did it once last time and didn't get hooked, so what's the harm in doing it again?' Does this ring any bells? They're falling into the same trap yet again!

Please be clear that this pattern only relates to the willpower method. When you quit with Easyway, you'll not feel deprived and you'll be completely free. You can relax from the moment you make the decision never to place another bet, since you know that you're not making any sacrifice and instead of interpreting the pangs of the Little Monster as 'I want to gamble' and then thinking, 'But I mustn't' or 'I can't', you say to yourself, 'This is what gamblers feel all the time. It's what keeps them gambling. Non-gamblers do not suffer this feeling. Isn't it marvellous, I am a non-gambler, and so the feeling will soon pass and I'll never have to suffer it again. YIPPEE, I'm free!'

Addicts who quit with the willpower method, on the other hand, are never quite sure whether they've kicked it.

THE MOMENT OF TRUTH – MAKE THE DECISION NEVER TO GAMBLE AGAIN

Soon you're going to become a non-gambler. If this thought makes you panic, remind yourself of these simple facts:

• The gambling industry depends on that panic to keep you hooked.

• Gambling doesn't relieve the panic, it causes it.

Take a moment to compose yourself. Do you really have any reason to panic? Nothing bad can possibly happen as a result of you stopping gambling. Terrible things will happen if you don't.

In a matter of days you'll feel stronger, both physically and mentally. You'll have more money, more energy, more confidence and more self-respect. Enjoy this wonderful freedom right from the start.

Waiting to see if they succeed is one of the reasons why gamblers who try to stop on the willpower method find it so difficult and why they never feel completely free.

You become a non-gambler the moment you stop gambling. What you're achieving is a new frame of mind, an understanding that gambling does nothing for you and that, by not gambling, you're freeing yourself from a life of slavery, misery and degradation.

Replace any panic you may have felt with a feeling of excitement and anticipation. You no longer need to be evasive, secretive or dishonest. You're about to discover the joy of having nothing to hide. Rejoice! This is going to be one of the best experiences you've ever had and it will have a major, positive impact on the length, quality and enjoyment of your future life.

YOU'RE ABOUT TO BECOME FREE!

SUMMARY

• The trauma of quitting on willpower is entirely psychological. Easyway involves neither willpower nor trauma.

• See the physical withdrawal as the death throes of the Little Monster and enjoy starving it to death.

• Gamblers suffer withdrawal pangs all the time. Non-gamblers don't suffer them at all.

• Get into a positive frame of mind: feel the excitement of what you're achieving.

Chapter 17

PREPARING TO QUIT

IN THIS CHAPTER
• *THE BEST TIME TO STOP* • *CHECK YOUR STATE OF MIND*
• *DO I HAVE TO OWN UP?*
• *WHAT IF I STILL HAVE BETS OUTSTANDING?*

You've been given nearly all the information you need to free yourself from gambling, easily, painlessly and permanently. Now you just have to choose your moment.

You should by now be feeling eager and excited about stopping and your frame of mind should be, 'Great! There's no reason to gamble any more.' We have reversed the brainwashing and dispelled the illusions that made you believe that gambling gave you pleasure and a crutch. We've replaced them with the reality: gambling does absolutely nothing for you whatsoever.

You have every reason to celebrate. You're about to walk free from an evil trap, which has kept you imprisoned and been ruining your life, making you miserable, confused, frightened and angry. You're about to reclaim control over your life and banish those feelings of slavery and powerlessness for good.

Very soon you'll be a non-gambler. You're about to discover the unbridled joy of having nothing to hide, having time for the people you love and the things you love to do, and being in control. While you were in the gambling trap you forgot how to enjoy the genuine pleasures in life. You're about to get that huge part of your life back.

YOU HAVE EVERY REASON TO BE OVERJOYED!

D-DAY

There are two typical occasions that tend to trigger attempts to quit. One is a traumatic event, such as your partner discovering your problem, or a financial blow. The other is a 'special' day, such as your birthday or New Year's Day. I call these 'meaningless days' because they have no bearing whatsoever on your gambling, other than providing a target date for you to make your attempt to stop. That would be fine if it helped, but meaningless days actually cause more harm than good.

Meaningless days encourage us to go through the damaging cycle of half-hearted attempts to quit, bringing on the feeling of deprivation, followed by the sense of failure that reinforces the belief that stopping is difficult, perhaps even impossible. And of course gamblers spend their lives looking for excuses to put off 'the dreaded day'. Meaningless days provide the perfect excuse to say, 'I will quit... just not today.'

Then there are the days when something shakes your world and you respond by saying it's time to sort yourself out. But these stressful times are also when your desire to gamble becomes strongest because you regard gambling as a form of crutch.

This is another ingenuity of the gambling trap:

NO MATTER WHICH DAY YOU CHOOSE TO QUIT, IT ALWAYS SEEMS TO BE WRONG

Some gamblers choose their annual holiday to quit, thinking that they'll be able to cope better away from the everyday stresses of work and home life and the usual temptations to gamble. Others pick a time when there are no big events coming up that might entice them to gamble.

These approaches might work for a while, but they leave a lingering doubt: 'OK, I've coped so far but what about when I go back to work or that big event comes round?'

When you quit with Easyway, we encourage you to go out and enjoy life and handle stress straight away, so that you can prove to yourself from the start that, even at times when you feared you would find it hard to cope without gambling, you're actually happy to be free.

So, what is the best time to quit? Imagine if you saw someone you love hurting themselves repeatedly. What would you say to them?

PLEASE STOP NOW!

That's what they would say to you if they knew about your gambling problem. You have everything you need to quit. Like an athlete on the blocks at the start of the Olympic 100 metres final, you're in peak condition to make the greatest achievement of your life RIGHT NOW!

Think of everything you have to gain. A life free from slavery, dishonesty, misery, anger, deceit and self-loathing! No more scratching around for money to feed your addiction; no more lying to people about what you need it for; no more hiding yourself away in darkened rooms late at night; no more coming away feeling disappointed, guilty and weak because your latest bout of gambling has failed to do you any good at all, just as, deep down, you knew it would.

> *You don't gamble to win. You gamble so you can gamble the next day.*
>
> **Bert Ambrose (musician)**

In place of all that misery you can look forward to living in the light, with your head held high, enjoying open, honest relationships with the people around you, feeling in control of how you spend your time and money, and finding enjoyment in the genuine pleasures that you enjoyed before you started gambling.

With so much happiness to gain and so much misery to rid yourself of, what possible reason is there to wait? It's time for my sixth instruction:

THE SEVENTH INSTRUCTION
DON'T WAIT TO QUIT. NOW IS THE RIGHT TIME

If this isn't how you feel, if you have doubts about what you're about to do, don't worry. It simply means that you haven't understood something and you need to go back and re-read it until you do. To help you, take a look at the code word,

RATIONALISED, on page 218. This serves as both a reminder and a checklist. Go through each item and ask yourself:

- Do I understand it?

- Do I agree with it?

- Am I following it?

If you have any doubts, re-read the relevant chapters.

STOPPING WITH EASYWAY IS EASY. ALL YOU NEED TO DO IS FOLLOW THE INSTRUCTIONS AND YOU'LL SUCCEED.

You have already done the hard work necessary to put yourself in the right frame of mind. Your training and preparation are almost complete.

You're fully equipped to succeed at something that most former gamblers regard as the most important and significant achievement of their lives.

IF YOU FEEL LIKE A DOG STRAINING AT THE LEASH, EAGER TO GET ON WITH IT, THAT'S GREAT, BUT YOU STILL NEED TO CONCENTRATE CAREFULLY ON THE REST OF THE BOOK.

R	**REJOICE!** *THERE'S NOTHING TO GIVE UP.*
A	**ADVICE** *IGNORE IT IF IT CONFLICTS WITH EASYWAY.*
T	**TIMING** *DO IT NOW!*
I	**ILLUSIONS** *REMOVE THEM ALL NOW AND YOU WILL BE FREE.*
O	**ONE BET** *IS ALL IT TAKES TO HOOK YOU AGAIN.*
N	**NEVER** *GAMBLE OR EVEN CRAVE GAMBLING.*
A	**ADDICTIVE PERSONALITY** *A THEORY THAT'S IRRELEVANT TO STOPPING.*
L	**LIFESTYLE** *REDISCOVER GENUINE PLEASURES.*
I	**IMMEDIATE** *YOU'RE FREE AS SOON AS YOU DECIDE TO BE.*
S	**SUBSTITUTES** *YOU'RE NOT 'GIVING UP' ANYTHING, SO YOU DON'T NEED ANY.*
E	**ELEPHANTS** *DON'T TRY NOT TO THINK ABOUT GAMBLING.*
D	**DOUBT** *NEVER DOUBT YOUR DECISION TO QUIT.*

TYING UP THE LOOSE ENDS

You'll soon be making the decision never to gamble again. Before you do so, it's important that you remove any lingering connections that might prevent you from becoming completely free. If you have an account with a betting firm, close it. And if you have any ongoing bets, cancel them.

The best way to do this is over the phone. Explain to them that you're completing treatment for gambling addiction and ask to close your account under self-exclusion. They should refund any balance you may have in your account and put an exclusion on you accessing the account, usually for a minimum period of six months. Ask for this to be permanent. If they're a reputable firm, they may talk to you about your addiction and steer you towards a help organisation. Tell them politely that you're already receiving the help you need.

If you have any bets still unresolved – for example, the winner of the next World Cup – ask to cancel them. They should return your stake and this will be included in any balance refunded on closure of your account. Should they decide that the stake isn't refundable, tell them you want to forgo any potential winnings anyway and put this in writing. It's essential that you don't retain any lingering interest in any bet you've placed. You're making a clean break.

Shocking fact

According to a study by the University of North Carolina at Wilmington, an estimated six per cent of American college students struggle with gambling problems.

COMING CLEAN

Many gamblers go to great lengths to conceal their problem. If you've kept your gambling problem secret from those close to you so far, the idea of coming clean about it now that it's over may seem like a non-starter. The prospect of owning up can be too daunting. You might decide it's best never to tell your friends or family, that they'd be better off not having to bear the burden of that knowledge.

> *A gambler never makes the same mistake twice. It is usually three or four times.*
>
> **V.P. Pappy**
> **(writer on poker)**

But please don't kid yourself. It's likely the people you think you've been deceiving haven't been deceived at all. They've probably noticed the change in your behaviour. They may have already been hurt by your irritability and become suspicious of your inability to apply yourself to work and other commitments. Furthermore, the dishonesty of being a secret gambler is a major cause of stress and owning up can be a great relief. If you choose to do so, you should tell them that you have read a book on stopping gambling and that you have now succeeded in quitting. Apologise for any hurt your gambling has caused them and vow to repair any damage, including repaying all your debts.

> *Gambling is a disease of barbarians, superficially civilised.*
> **Dean Inge**
> *(academic)*

Be aware that the people you're owning up to could react with hurt and anger at first, but in the long run they're likely to respect you for coming clean. It also gives them the opportunity to understand why your behaviour has changed and may help you to re-establish better relationships with them. You may even find they're relieved by your admission.

Added to which:

ANY SENSE OF SHAME OR EMBARRASSMENT YOU FEEL ABOUT OWNING UP WILL BE HUGELY OUTWEIGHED BY THE RELIEF AT NO LONGER HAVING TO LIE

But if you feel that your loved ones aren't ready for the full story of your gambling addiction and that 'dumping it on them' would be unfair, that's fine. You're the best person to judge this. Once you're enjoying the confidence and self-respect that comes with your newfound freedom, you'll be better equipped to work out the best way to deal with this issue.

SUMMARY

- The time to stop is now. There's no reason to wait.
- Close any betting accounts and cancel all outstanding bets.
- Think carefully about telling family and friends.
- Remember the checklist, RATIONALISED.

Chapter 18

BECOMING A HAPPY NON-GAMBLER

You'll soon be making a solemn vow never to gamble again.
You will then be free.

This is a momentous occasion in your life and one of the most important decisions you'll ever make. You're freeing yourself from slavery and achieving something marvellous, something that others will admire and respect you for. And most important of all, you'll go right up in the estimation of one person in particular: yourself.

In order to complete this marvellous transformation in your life, you need to make a solemn vow that you'll never place another bet.

You've reached a stage that often strikes panic into gamblers, smokers, alcoholics and other addicts: the moment when they decide to stop. If you find the prospect unnerving, don't worry. It's completely normal to feel nervous at this stage and it's no threat to your chances of success.

You now have all the knowledge and understanding that you need to become a happy non-gambler easily, painlessly and permanently.

You've nothing to fear. The only thing that is facing sudden death is your gambling problem. You're not losing a friend; you have no reason to grieve. On the contrary, you should rejoice in the death of your mortal enemy.

You had no need to gamble before you started; you've no need to gamble now. In fact, you've already stopped. All that's left to do is to cement the moment in your mind when you commit to becoming a happy non-gambler for life.

Remind yourself that you're not 'giving up' anything. Lifelong non-gamblers and ex-gamblers – most of the people in the world – are quite happy without gambling. What pleasure does it give? What support does it provide? What does it do for you? If you've followed and understood everything in this book, you'll come to the obvious conclusion:

NOTHING AT ALL

IN HER OWN WORDS: CLAIRE

I wish I could put into words the incredible joy I felt when I realised I no longer needed to gamble. It was an enormous relief. I felt like a dark cloud had been lifted from my life. I realised I had come to despise myself,

> I was permanently worried about all the money I'd squandered and where I was going to get my next stake from, and the effect it was having on my relationships with my husband and children terrified me. Suddenly those worries were gone. I no longer felt weak, dishonest, irritable, hopeless – a failed mum. I felt like a winner.

You should now be feeling excited about finally ending the misery that gambling has caused you. You're about to escape from a fiendish trap and achieve something marvellous.

I now want you to think about gambling. Think about the misery it has caused you and how helpless you felt when you were in the gambling trap, wanting to quit but unable to do so. Think about the hours you've wasted and the money you've squandered. Most of all think about the constant lack of fulfilment that has kept you chasing an impossible goal.

Now think about everything you're about to gain by quitting. More time, more money, more freedom. Think how good it will feel not to despise yourself for your lack of control. Think of the relief of being able to live your life free from deceit and guilt. Most of all, think how good it will feel not to be a slave.

THE DECISION

Very soon I will ask you to make a solemn vow that you'll never gamble again. Before you do, it's essential that you're completely clear that gambling gives you no pleasure or crutch whatsoever and, therefore, you're not making any sacrifice at all and there's no reason to feel deprived.

The decision never to gamble again is one of the most important decisions you'll ever make because the quality of your future life critically depends on it, and I can't believe there's anything more important to you than that. With other important decisions, such as which partner or job you choose, you can never be sure they're correct. You may not regret them later and you may be perfectly happy with them, but you can never know what would have happened if you had made a different choice. The beauty of the decision you're about to make now is that not only do you know that it's of critical importance, but you can also be 100 per cent certain that it's the correct decision, even as you make it.

Nothing bad is happening in your life. On the contrary, something marvellous is happening. It's one of the rare occasions when there's absolutely nothing to lose and everything to gain: no downside and a huge upside. You're making marvellous positive gains and what are you giving up? ABSOLUTELY NOTHING. So cast aside any feelings of doom or gloom and approach the process with a feeling of excitement, of relief that whole nightmare is now finally over and of elation that you're now free.

THE EIGHTH INSTRUCTION
MAKE A DECISION NEVER TO GAMBLE AGAIN AND
NEVER EVEN BEGIN TO QUESTION THAT DECISION

It's only the questioning or doubting of that decision that can possibly make it difficult for you to stop. If you find the thought of never gambling again difficult to accept, try taking on board the only alternative: to spend the rest of your life as a gambling slave.

Now take a deep breath and make that solemn vow. Be certain about the decision you're making, embrace the moment and greet it with a sense of triumph. 'Yes! I'm a non-gambler. I'm FREE!'

DON'T WAIT FOR ANYTHING TO HAPPEN

You're free from the moment you decide that you will never gamble again. That decision marks the start of your new life. There's nothing to wait for. You're now a non-gambler. Congratulations! You have taken the decision to walk away from slavery, misery, dishonesty and hopelessness. Freedom starts here.

Enjoy your victory. This is one of the greatest achievements of your life. It's important that this moment is firmly implanted in your mind. Right now you're fired up with powerful reasons to stop, but as the days, weeks and years slip by, your memory of how you were feeling about gambling today will dim. So fix those thoughts in your mind now while they're still vivid, so that even if your memory of the details should diminish, your recollection of what a nightmare it was to be a gambler does not.

CONGRATULATIONS! YOU'RE READY TO START ENJOYING LIFE AS A NON-GAMBLER!

KEEPING THE RIGHT MINDSET

You'll soon find it difficult to believe that you ever felt the need to gamble, let alone how much it controlled your life. This is a marvellous feeling and you should enjoy it. However, don't be fooled into the trap of thinking, 'I'm free now. Just one bet can't do any harm.' You might have moments when you're on a high, surrounded by gamblers, or you might suffer a trauma and your guard may drop. Prepare yourself for these situations now and make it part of your vow that, if and when they come, you'll be ready with the right mindset, so there's no way you'll be fooled into gambling again.

THE NINTH INSTRUCTION
ALWAYS REMEMBER, THERE'S NO SUCH THING AS 'JUST ONE BET'

If you place one bet, whether you win or lose, you'll place another and another and another and you'll quickly find yourself back in the trap.

You stopped because you didn't like life as a gambler, so instead of thinking, 'I must never gamble again,' think, 'This is great! I don't ever need to waste my time and money on making myself miserable again. I'M FREE!'

FREEDOM STARTS HERE!

SUMMARY

- Don't worry about last-minute nerves – they're completely normal.
- Make your decision to stop and never doubt it.
- You're free as soon as you make your vow.
- There's nothing to wait for. Enjoy being free right from the start.

Chapter 19

ENJOYING LIFE FREE FROM GAMBLING

IN THIS CHAPTER
- *THE FIRST FEW DAYS* • *ALL YOU HAVE GAINED*
- *COPING WITH BAD DAYS*
- *STAYING FREE FOREVER*

Well done! You're now ready to get on and enjoy the marvellous pleasures of life free from gambling.

For a few days, you may sense the cries of the Little Monster as it goes through its death throes. This is nothing more than your mind and body readjusting to the withdrawal from gambling. There's no need to fear it. Nor should you try to ignore it. Instead, recognise it for what it is: a sure sign that the monster that has had you in its clutches is dying, and rejoice that you are now back in control. Stopping gambling is a major positive change in your life. As with any other major positive change, such as moving to a new and better job or home, there can be an initial feeling of slight disorientation as you adjust to your new and improved circumstances. Don't worry if this happens, it's perfectly natural and need not undermine your success in any way.

People who try to quit with the willpower method respond to the death throes of the Little Monster by thinking, 'I want to gamble but

I must fight this desire', which makes them feel deprived, frustrated and insecure.

Of course, these feelings are not physically painful, but they can cause panic as they fear that the craving will never go and they'll have to carry on fighting the desire to gamble for the rest of their life. In reality, the death throes of the Little Monster are very slight and only last for a few days. They only become a problem if you start to worry about them or interpret them as a need or desire to gamble. If you feel them, picture a Little Monster searching around the desert for a drink when you have control of the water supply. All you have to do is keep the tap turned off and let it die of thirst. It's as easy as that.

Instead of thinking, 'I want to gamble but I'm not allowed to,' think, 'This is the Little Monster demanding its fix. This is what gamblers suffer throughout their gambling lives. Non-gamblers don't suffer this feeling. Isn't it great! I'm a non-gambler and soon I'll soon be free of it forever.' Think this way and those withdrawal pangs become moments of pleasure.

Remind yourself that there's no physical pain and that the only discomfort you might be feeling isn't because you've stopped gambling but because you started in the first place. Also be clear that gambling again, far from relieving that discomfort, would ensure that you suffered it for the rest of your life.

Take pleasure in starving that Little Monster. Revel in its death throes. Feel no guilt about rejoicing in its death; after all, it's been costing you a fortune, keeping you a slave and ruining your life for long enough.

START LIVING NOW

You don't have to wait for the Little Monster to die before you start enjoying life as a non-gambler. In fact, you don't have to wait for anything. Freedom began the moment you made your vow never to gamble again.

IT'S TIME TO GET ON WITH LIFE

One of the fantastic benefits of becoming a non-gambler is that you rediscover the joy of life's genuine pleasures. People in the gambling trap lose the ability to enjoy the things that non-gamblers enjoy most: reading books, watching entertainment, social occasions, relaxation, exercise, sex, etc. Now that you're a non-gambler, you have all these pleasures to get excited about again.

You'll find that situations you have come to regard as tedious or even irritating become enjoyable again: things like spending time with your loved ones, going for walks, seeing friends. Work too will become more enjoyable, as you find you're better able to concentrate, think clearly and handle stress.

There are so many marvellous gains to stopping gambling for good and the beauty is you can start enjoying them straight away because you are already:

FREE!

BAD DAYS

Everybody, gamblers and non-gamblers alike, has days when everything that can go wrong seems to. It has nothing to do with the fact that you've stopped gambling. In fact, when you stop you find that the bad days don't come around so frequently and seem much easier to deal with when they do.

For people who quit with the willpower method, bad days can be the trigger that leads to their downfall. Because they don't understand how the addiction works, even long after the physical withdrawal has ended they'll misinterpret normal feelings of stress or irritability as a need or desire to gamble. They find themselves in a difficult situation: they want to be a non-gambler, but they also want to gamble. They won't want to take up gambling again because they've made a huge effort to quit, so they'll feel deprived and that will make the stress and irritability worse.

Sooner or later their willpower will give out and they will succumb to the craving. They'll tell themselves it's 'just the once', but very soon they'll find themselves hooked again.

You might well find that when you have bad days, the thought of gambling enters your mind. Don't worry about it and don't try to push it to one side either. Remember the elephants! We cannot force our brains not to think about something. If you try *not* to think about gambling, you'll get frustrated and miserable. Instead, enjoy thinking about it. Rather than thinking, 'I mustn't gamble' or, 'I can't', think, 'Great! I'm a non-gambler! Yippee! I'm free!'

It's essential that you never doubt or question your decision to stop. Never make the mistake, that people on the willpower method make, of craving another bet. If you do you'll put yourself in the same impossible position as them: miserable if you don't gamble and even more miserable if you do.

THE TENTH INSTRUCTION
NEVER EVER GAMBLE AGAIN

Prepare yourself for the occasional bad day which will be nothing to do with having stopped gambling. Have your mindset ready. Protect yourself against getting caught out. Be ready for stress and remind yourself that you're better equipped to handle it as a non-gambler. Gambling would only make it worse.

Be absolutely clear there's no such thing as 'just one bet'. If the thought of having 'just one bet' ever occurs to you, instead of thinking, 'I mustn't', get it clearly into your mind that if you place 'just one bet', you'll place another and another and another. This is how you fell into the trap in the first place, so the question you need to ask yourself is, 'Do I want to become a gambler again and spend the rest of my life never being allowed to stop?'

Cast your mind back to what it was like to be a gambler – you didn't like it or you wouldn't have decided to stop. This is a vital point to remember. Then cast your mind back over how marvellous life has been since you quit and how relieved you were when you realised you no longer needed to do it and rejoice in the thought: 'Yippee! I'm a non-gambler! I'm free.' Such occasions will then be moments of pleasure when you congratulate yourself that you've done it and you'll enjoy being a non-gambler for the rest of your life.

SUMMARY

- Enjoy the death throes of the Little Monster.
- Start enjoying life as a non-gambler right from square one.
- Be prepared for bad days – you'll handle them better as a non-gambler.
- NEVER EVER GAMBLE AGAIN.

Chapter 20

USEFUL REMINDERS

From time to time you may find it useful to remind yourself of some of the issues that we've discussed. The key points are summarised here, together with a reminder of the instructions. Follow these and you'll remain a happy non-gambler for the rest of your life.

- Don't wait for anything. You're already a non-gambler from the moment you make your decision to quit. You've cut off the supply to the Little Monster and unlocked the door of your prison.

- Accept that gamblers and non-gamblers have the occasional bad day, maybe to do with an argument at home or a problem at work. These will have nothing to do with you having stopped gambling. You'll always have the consolation on those days of being a happy non-gambler. Because you'll be stronger both physically and mentally within no time at all, you'll enjoy the good times more and handle the bad times better.

- Be aware that a very important change is happening in your life. Like all major changes, including those for the better, it can take time to adjust. Don't worry if you feel different or disoriented for a few days. Just accept it and remind yourself how lucky you are to be free.

• Remember you've stopped gambling, you haven't stopped living. You can now start enjoying life to the full.

• There's no need to avoid gamblers. Go out and enjoy social occasions and show yourself you can handle stress right from the start.

• Don't envy gamblers. When you're with gamblers, remember you're not being deprived, they are.

• Don't substitute gambling with anything else. You're losing nothing, so you don't need a substitute.

• Politely refuse when friends offer to 'bail you out'. It's up to you to solve the problem with Easyway.

• Never doubt or question your decision to stop – you know it's the right one. Never crave another bet. If you do, you'll put yourself in an impossible position: you'll be miserable if you don't and even more miserable if you do.

• Make sure right from the start that if the thought of 'just one bet' ever enters your mind, you think, 'Great!

I'm a non-gambler.' Enjoy being free.

• Don't try *not* to think about gambling, it doesn't work. By trying to, you'll make yourself frustrated and miserable. It's easy to think about gambling without feeling miserable: instead of thinking, 'I mustn't gamble,' think, 'YIPPEE! I'M FREE!'

THE INSTRUCTIONS

1. Follow all the instructions.

2. Keep an open mind.

3. Start with a feeling of elation.

4. Ignore all advice and influences that conflict with Easyway.

5. Resist any promise of a temporary fix.

6. Get it clear in your mind: gambling gives you no genuine pleasure or crutch; you are not making a sacrifice; there is nothing to give up and no reason to feel deprived.

7. Don't wait to quit. Do it now!

8. Make a decision never to gamble again and never question it.

9. Always remember there's no such thing as 'just one bet'

10. Never gamble again.

ALLEN CARR'S EASYWAY CLINICS

The following list indicates the countries where Allen Carr's Easyway To Stop Smoking Clinics are currently operational.

Check www.allencarr.com for latest additions to this list.

The success rate at the clinics, based on the three-month money-back guarantee, is over 90 per cent.

Selected clinics also offer sessions that deal with alcohol, other drugs and weight issues. Please check with your nearest clinic, listed below, for details.

Allen Carr's Easyway guarantee that you will find it easy to stop at the clinics or your money back.

JOIN US!

Allen Carr's Easyway Clinics have spread throughout the world with incredible speed and success. Our global franchise network now covers more than 150 cities in over 45 countries. This amazing growth has been achieved entirely organically. Former addicts, just like you, were so impressed by the ease with which they stopped that they felt inspired to contact us to see how they could bring the method to their region.

If you feel the same, contact us for details on how to become an Allen Carr's Easyway To Stop Smoking or an Allen Carr's Easyway To Stop Drinking franchisee.

Email us at: **join-us@allencarr.com** including your full name, postal address and region of interest.

SUPPORT US!

No, don't send us money!

You have achieved something really marvellous. Every time we hear of someone escaping from the sinking ship, we get a feeling of enormous satisfaction.

It would give us great pleasure to hear that you have freed yourself from the slavery of addiction so please visit the following web page where you can tell us of your success, inspire others to follow in your footsteps and hear about ways you can help to spread the word.

www.allencarr.com/fanzone

You can "like" our facebook page here
www.facebook.com/AllenCarr

Together, we can help further Allen Carr's mission: to cure the world of addiction.

CLINICS

LONDON CLINIC AND WORLDWIDE HEAD OFFICE
Park House, 14 Pepys Road,
Raynes Park, London SW20 8NH
Tel: +44 (0)20 8944 7761
Fax: +44 (0)20 8944 8619
Email: mail@allencarr.com
Website: www.allencarr.com
Therapists: John Dicey, Colleen Dwyer,
Crispin Hay, Emma Hudson, Rob
Fielding, Sam Kelser, Sam Cleary

Worldwide Press Office
Contact: John Dicey
Tel: +44 (0)7970 88 44 52
Email: media@allencarr.com

UK Clinic Information and Central Booking Line
Tel: 0800 389 2115 (UK only)

UK CLINICS

Birmingham
Tel & Fax: +44 (0)121 423 1227
Therapists: John Dicey, Colleen Dwyer,
Crispin Hay, Rob Fielding
Email: mail@allencarr.com
Website: www.allencarr.com

Brentwood
Tel: 0800 028 7257
Therapists: John Dicey, Colleen Dwyer,
Emma Hudson, Sam Kelser
Email: mail@allencarr.com
Website: www.allencarr.com

Brighton
Tel: 0800 028 7257
Therapists: John Dicey, Colleen Dwyer,
Emma Hudson
Email: mail@allencarr.com
Website: www.allencarr.com

Bristol
Tel: 0800 028 7257
Therapists: John Dicey, Colleen Dwyer,
Emma Hudson, Sam Kelser
Email: mail@allencarr.com
Website: www.allencarr.com

Cambridge
Tel: +44 (0)20 8944 7761
Therapists: Emma Hudson, Sam Kelser
Email: mail@allencarr.com
Website: www.allencarr.com

Coventry
Tel: 0800 321 3007
Therapist: Rob Fielding
Email: info@easywaycoventry.co.uk
Website: www.allencarr.com

Crewe
Tel: +44 (0)1270 664176
Therapist: Debbie Brewer-West
Email: debbie@easyway2stopsmoking.co.uk
Website: www.allencarr.com

Cumbria
Tel: 0800 077 6187
Therapist: Mark Keen
Email: mark@easywaycumbria.co.uk
Website: www.allencarr.com

Derby
Tel: +44 (0)1270 664176
Therapist: Debbie Brewer-West
Email: debbie@easyway2stopsmoking.co.uk
Website: www.allencarr.com

Guernsey
Tel: 0800 077 6187
Therapist: Mark Keen
Email: mark@easywaylancashire.co.uk
Website: www.allencarr.com

Isle of Man
Tel: 0800 077 6187
Therapist: Mark Keen
Email: mark@easywaylancashire.co.uk
Website: www.allencarr.com

Jersey
Tel: 0800 077 6187
Therapist: Mark Keen
Email: mark@easywaylancashire.co.uk
Website: www.allencarr.com

Kent
Tel: 0800 028 7257
Therapists: John Dicey, Colleen Dwyer,
Emma Hudson, Sam Kelser
Email: mail@allencarr.com
Website: www.allencarr.com

Lancashire
Tel: 0800 077 6187
Therapist: Mark Keen
Email: mark@easywaylancashire.co.uk
Website: www.allencarr.com

Leeds
Tel: 0800 077 6187
Therapist: Mark Keen
Email: mark@easywayyorkshire.co.uk
Website: www.allencarr.com

Leicester
Tel: 0800 321 3007
Therapist: Rob Fielding
Email: info@easywayleicester.co.uk
Website: www.allencarr.com

Lincoln
Tel: 0800 321 3007
Therapist: Rob Fielding
Email: info@easywayleicester.co.uk
Website: www.allencarr.com

Liverpool
Tel: 0800 077 6187
Therapist: Mark Keen
Email: mark@easywayliverpool.co.uk
Website: www.allencarr.com

Manchester
Tel: 0800 077 6187
Therapist: Mark Keen
Email: mark@easywaymanchester.com
Website: www.allencarr.com

Manchester—alcohol sessions
Tel: +44 (0)7936 712942
Therapist: Mike Connolly
Email: info@stopdrinkingnorth.co.uk
Website: www.allencarr.com

Milton Keynes
Tel: +44 (0)20 8944 7761
Therapists: Emma Hudson, Sam Kelser
Email: mail@allencarr.com
Website: www.allencarr.com

Newcastle/North East
Tel: 0800 077 6187
Therapist: Mark Keen
Email: mark@easywaynortheast.co.uk
Website: www.allencarr.com

Northern Ireland/Belfast
Tel: 0800 077 6187
Therapist: Mark Keen
Email: mark@easywaycumbria.co.uk
Website: www.allencarr.com

Nottingham
Tel: +44 (0)1270 664176
Therapist: Debbie Brewer-West
Email: debbie@easyway2stopsmoking.co.uk
Website: www.allencarr.com

Reading
Tel: 0800 028 7257
Therapists: John Dicey, Colleen Dwyer,
Emma Hudson
Email: info@allencarr.com
Website: www.allencarr.com

SCOTLAND
Glasgow and Edinburgh
Tel: +44 (0)131 449 7858
Therapists: Paul Melvin and Jim
McCreadie

Email: info@easywayscotland.co.uk
Website: www.allencarr.com

Sheffield
Tel: +44 (0)1924 830768
Therapist: Joseph Spencer
Email: joseph@easywaysheffield.co.uk
Website: www.allencarr.com

Shrewsbury
Tel: +44 (0)1270 664176
Therapist: Debbie Brewer-West
Email: debbie@easyway2stopsmoking.
co.uk
Website: www.allencarr.com

Southampton
Tel: 0800 028 7257
Therapists: John Dicey, Colleen Dwyer,
Emma Hudson
Email: mail@allencarr.com
Website: www.allencarr.com

Southport
Tel: 0800 077 6187
Therapist: Mark Keen
Email: mark@easywaylancashire.co.uk
Website: www.allencarr.com

Staines/Heathrow
Tel: 0800 028 7257
Therapists: John Dicey, Colleen Dwyer,
Emma Hudson
Email: mail@allencarr.com
Website: www.allencarr.com

Stevenage
Tel: +44 (0)20 8944 7761
Therapists: Emma Hudson, Sam Kelser
Email: mail@allencarr.com
Website: www.allencarr.com

Stoke
Tel: +44 (0)1270 664176
Therapist: Debbie Brewer-West
Email: debbie@easyway2stopsmoking.
co.uk
Website: www.allencarr.com

Surrey
Park House, 14 Pepys Road, Raynes Park,
London SW20 8NH
Tel: +44 (0)20 8944 7761
Fax: +44 (0)20 8944 8619
Therapists: John Dicey, Colleen Dwyer,
Crispin Hay, Emma Hudson, Rob Fielding,
Sam Kelser
Email: mail@allencarr.com
Website: www.allencarr.com

Swindon
Tel: 0800 028 7257
Therapists: John Dicey, Colleen Dwyer,
Emma Hudson, Sam Kelser
Email: mail@allencarr.com
Website: www.allencarr.com

Telford
Tel: +44 (0)1270 664176
Therapist: Debbie Brewer-West
Email: debbie@easyway2stopsmoking.co.uk
Website: www.allencarr.com

Watford
Tel: +44 (0)20 8944 7761
Therapists: Emma Hudson, Sam Kelser
Email: mail@allencarr.com
Website: www.allencarr.com

WORLDWIDE CLINICS

REPUBLIC OF IRELAND
Dublin and Cork
Lo-Call (From ROI) 1 890 ESYWAY (37 99 29)
Tel: +353 (0)1 499 9010 (4 lines)
Therapists: Brenda Sweeney and Team
Email: info@allencarr.ie
Website: www.allencarr.com

AUSTRALIA
ACT, NSW, NT, QSL, VIC
Tel: 1300 848 028
Therapist: Natalie Clays
Email: natalie@allencarr.com.au
Website: www.allencarr.com

South Australia
Tel: 1300 848 028
Therapist: Jaime Reed
Email: sa@allencarr.au
Website: www.allencarr.com

Western Australia
Tel: 1300 848 0281
Therapist: Dianne Fisher
Email: wa@allencarr.com.au
Website: www.allencarr.com

AUSTRIA
Sessions held throughout Austria
Freephone: 0800RAUCHEN
(0800 7282436)
Tel: +43 (0)3512 44755
Therapists: Erich Kellermann and Team
Email: info@allen-carr.at
Website: www.allencarr.com

BELGIUM
Antwerp
Tel: +32 (0)3 281 6255
Fax: +32 (0)3 744 0608
Therapist: Dirk Nielandt
Email: info@allencarr.be
Website: www.allencarr.com

BRAZIL
São Paulo
Therapists: Alberto Steinberg &
Lilian Brunstein
Email: contato@easywaysp.com.br
Tel Lilian - (55) (11) 99456-0153
Tel Alberto - (55) (11) 99325-6514
Website: www.allencarr.com

BULGARIA
Tel: 0800 14104 / +359 899 88 99 07
Therapist: Rumyana Kostadinova
Email: rk@nepushaveche.com
Website: www.allencarr.com

CHILE
Tel: +56 2 4744587
Therapist: Claudia Sarmiento

Email: contacto@allencarr.cl
Website: www.allencarr.com

COLOMBIA – Bogota (South America)
Therapist: Felipe Sanint Echeverri
Tel: +57 3158681043
E-mail: info@nomascigarillos.com
Website: www.allencarr.com

CZECH REPUBLIC
Tel: +420 234 261 787
Therapist: Dagmar Janecková
Email: dagmar.janeckova@allencarr.cz
Website: www.allencarr.com

DENMARK
Sessions held throughout Denmark
Tel: +45 70267711
Therapist: Mette Fonss
Email: mette@easyway.dk
Website: www.allencarr.com

ESTONIA
Tel: +372 733 0044
Therapist: Henry Jakobson
Email: info@allencarr.ee
Website: www.allencarr.com

FINLAND
Tel: +358-(0)45 3544099
Therapist: Janne Ström
Email: info@allencarr.fi
Website: www.allencarr.com

FRANCE
Sessions held throughout France
Freephone: 0800 386387
Tel: +33 (4) 91 33 54 55
Email: info@allencarr.fr
Website: www.allencarr.com

GERMANY
Sessions held throughout Germany
Freephone: 08000RAUCHEN
(0800 07282436)
Tel: +49 (0) 8031 90190-0
Therapists: Erich Kellermann and Team

Email: info@allen-carr.de
Website: www.allencarr.com

GREECE
Sessions held throughout Greece
Tel: +30 210 5224087
Therapist: Panos Tzouras
Email: panos@allencarr.gr
Website: www.allencarr.com

GUATEMALA
Tel: +502 2362 0000
Therapist: Michelle Binford
Email: bienvenid@dejedefumarfacil.com
Website: www.allencarr.com

HONG KONG
Email: info@easywayhongkong.com
Website: www.allencarr.com

HUNGARY
Seminars in Budapest and 12 other cities
across Hungary
Tel: 06 80 624 426 (freephone) or
+36 20 580 9244
Therapist: Gabor Szasz
Email: szasz.gabor@allencarr.hu
Website: www.allencarr.com

ICELAND
Reykjavik
Tel: +354 588 7060
Therapist: Petur Einarsson
Email: easyway@easyway.is
Website: www.allencarr.com

INDIA
Bangalore & Chennai
Tel: +91 (0)80 41603838
Therapist: Suresh Shottam
Email: info@easywaytostopsmoking.co.in
Website: www.allencarr.com

IRAN—opening 2018
Tehran and Mashhad
Website: www.allencarr.com

ISRAEL
Sessions held throughout Israel
Tel: +972 (0)3 6212525
Therapists: Ramy Romanovsky,
Orit Rozen
Email: info@allencarr.co.il
Website: www.allencarr.com

ITALY
Sessions held throughout Italy
Tel/Fax: +39 (0)2 7060 2438
Therapists: Francesca Cesati and Team
Email: info@easywayitalia.com
Website: www.allencarr.com

JAPAN
Sessions held throughout Japan
www.allencarr.com

LEBANON
Mob: **+961 76 789555**
Therapist: Sadek El-Assaad
Email: stopsmoking@allencarreasyway.me
Website: www.allencarr.com

LITHUANIA
Tel: +370 694 29591
Therapist: Evaldas Zvirblis
Email: info@mestirukyti.eu
Website: www.allencarr.com

MAURITIUS
Tel: +230 5727 5103
Therapist: Heidi Hoareau
Email: info@allencarr.mu
Website: www.allencarr.com

MEXICO
Sessions held throughout Mexico
Tel: +52 55 2623 0631
Therapists: Jorge Davo and Mario
Campuzano Otero
Email: info@allencarr-mexico.com
Website: www.allencarr.com

NETHERLANDS
Sessions held throughout the
Netherlands
Allen Carr's Easyway 'stoppen met
roken'
Tel: (+31)53 478 43 62 /
(+31)900 786 77 37
Email: info@allencarr.nl
Website: www.allencarr.com

NEW ZEALAND
North Island – Auckland
Tel: +64 (0)9 817 5396
Therapist: Vickie Macrae
Email: vickie@easywaynz.co.nz
Website: www.allencarr.com

South Island – Dunedin and
Invercargill
Tel: 027 4139 381
Therapist: Debbie Kinder
Email: easywaysouth@icloud.com
Website: www.allencarr.com

NORWAY
Oslo
Tel: +47 93 20 09 11
Therapist: René Adde
Email: post@easyway-norge.no
Website: www.allencarr.com

PERU
Lima
Tel: +511 637 7310
Therapist: Luis Loranca
Email: lloranca@dejardefumaraltoque.com
Website: www.allencarr.com

POLAND
Sessions held throughout Poland
Tel: +48 (0)22 621 36 11
Therapist: Anna Kabat
Email: info@allen-carr.pl
Website: www.allencarr.com

PORTUGAL
Oporto
Tel: +351 22 9958698
Therapist: Ria Slof
Email: info@comodeixardefumar.com
Website: www.allencarr.com

ROMANIA
Tel: +40 (0) 7321 3 8383
Therapist: Diana Vasiliu
Email: raspunsuri@allencarr.ro
Website: www.allencarr.com

RUSSIA
Moscow
Tel: +7 495 644 64 26
Therapist: Alexander Formin
Email: info@allencarr.ru
Website: www.allencarr.com

Crimea, Simferopol
Tel: +38 095 781 8180
Therapist: Yuriy Zhvakolyuk
Email: zhvakolyuk@gmail.com
Website: www.allencarr.com

St Petersburg
Website: www.allencarr.com

SERBIA
Belgrade
Tel: +381 (0)11 308 8686
Email: office@allencarr.co.rs
Website: www.allencarr.com

SINGAPORE
Tel: +65 6329 9660
Therapist: Pam Oei
Email: pam@allencarr.com.sg
Website: www.allencarr.com

SLOVAKIA
Tel: +421 233 04 69 92
Therapist: Peter Sánta
Email: peter.santa@allencarr.sk
Website: www.allencarr.com

SLOVENIA
Tel: 00386 (0) 40 77 61 77
Therapist: Gregor Server
Email: easyway@easyway.si
Website: www.allencarr.com

SOUTH AFRICA
Sessions held throughout South Africa
National Booking Line: 0861 100 200
Head Office: 15 Draper Square,
Draper St, Claremont 7708, Cape Town
Cape Town: Dr Charles Nel
Tel: +27 (0)21 851 5883
Mobile: 083 600 5555
Therapists: Dr Charles Nel, Malcolm
Robinson and Team
Email: easyway@allencarr.co.za
Website: www.allencarr.com

SOUTH KOREA
Seoul
Tel: +82 (0)70 4227 1862
Therapist: Yousung Cha
Email: master@allencarr.co.kr
Website: www.allencarr.com

SWEDEN
Tel: +46 70 695 6850
Therapists: Nina Ljungqvist,
Renée Johansson
Email: info@easyway.se
Website: www.allencarr.com

SWITZERLAND
Sessions held throughout Switzerland
Freephone: 0800RAUCHEN
(0800/728 2436)
Tel: +41 (0)52 383 3773
Fax: +41 (0)52 3833774
Therapists: Cyrill Argast and Team
For sessions in Suisse Romand and
Svizzera Italiana:
Tel: 0800 386 387
Email: info@allen-carr.ch
Website: www.allencarr.com

TURKEY
Sessions held throughout Turkey
Tel: +90 212 358 5307
Therapist: Emre Ustunucar
Email: info@allencarrturkiye.com
Website: www.allencarr.com

UKRAINE
Kiev
Tel: +38 044 353 2934
Therapist: Kirill Stekhin
Email: kirill@allencarr.kiev.ua
Website: www.allencarr.com

UNITED ARAB EMIRATES
Dubai and Abu Dhabi
Tel: +971 56 693 4000
Therapist: Sadek El-Assaad
Email: iwanttoquit@allencarreasyway.me
Website: www.allencarr.com

USA
Denver
Toll free: 1 866 666 4299 /
New York: 212- 330 9194
Email: info@theeasywaytostopsmoking.com
Website: www.allencarr.com
Therapists: Damian O'Hara, Collene
Curran, David Skeist

Houston
Toll free: 1 866 666 4299 / New York:
212- 330 9194
Email: info@theeasywaytostopsmoking.com
Website: www.allencarr.com
Therapists: Damian O'Hara, Collene
Curran, David Skeist

Los Angeles
Toll free: 1 866 666 4299 / New York:
212- 330 9194
Email: info@theeasywaytostopsmoking.com
Website: www.allencarr.com
Therapists: Damian O'Hara, Collene
Curran, David Skeist

Milwaukee (and South Wisconsin) —
Tel: +1 262 770 1260
Therapist: Wayne Spaulding
Email: wayne@easywaywisconsin.com
Website: www.allencarr.com

New Jersey — opening 2018
Website: www.allencarr.com

New York
Toll free: 1 866 666 4299 /
New York: 212- 330 9194
Email: info@theeasywaytostopsmoking.
com
Website: www.allencarr.com

Therapists: Damian O'Hara, Collene
Curran, David Skeist

CANADA
Sessions held throughout Canada
Toll free: +1-866 666 4299 /
+1 905 849 7736
English Therapist: Damian O'Hara
French Therapist: Rejean Belanger
Email: info@theeasywaytostopsmoking.
com
Website: www.allencarr.com

OTHER ALLEN CARR PUBLICATIONS

Allen Carr's revolutionary Easyway method is available in a wide variety of formats, including digitally as audiobooks and ebooks, and has been successfully applied to a broad range of subjects.

For more information about Easyway publications, please visit
shop.allencarr.com

Stop Smoking with Allen Carr
(with 70-minute audio CD)

Stop Smoking Now
(with hypnotherapy CD)

**Your Personal
Stop Smoking Plan**

The Easy Way to Stop Smoking

The Easy Way for Women to Stop Smoking

Easyway Express: Stop Smoking and Quit E-cigarettes
(ebook)

The Only Way to Stop Smoking Permanently

The Illustrated Easy Way to Stop Smoking

The Illustrated Easy Way for Women to Stop Smoking

The Nicotine Conspiracy
(ebook)

How to Be a Happy Nonsmoker
(ebook)

No More Ashtrays

Finally Free!

How to Stop Your Child Smoking

The Little Book of Quitting

Smoking Sucks (Parent Guide with 16 page pull-out comic)
(ebook)

Stop Drinking Now
(with hypnotherapy CD)

The Easy Way to Control Alcohol

Your Personal Stop Drinking Plan

The Illustrated Easy Way to Stop Drinking

The Easy Way for Women to Stop Drinking

No More Hangovers

Lose Weight Now
(with hypnotherapy CD)

No More Diets

The Easy Way for Women to Lose Weight

Good Sugar Bad Sugar

The Easy Way to Quit Sugar

No More Gambling
(ebook)

Get Out of Debt Now

No More Debt

The Easy Way to Enjoy Flying

No More Fear of Flying

Burning Ambition

No More Worrying

Packing It In The Easy Way
(the autobiography)

Want Easyway on your **smartphone** or **tablet**?
Search for "Allen Carr" in your app store.

Easyway publications are also available as audiobooks.
Visit **shop.allencarr.com** to find out more.